GENEALOGY TIPS & QUIPS

ELIZA WATSON

ISBN ebook: 978-1-950786-02-2

ISBN print book: 978-1-950786-03-9

❀ Created with Vellum

CONTENTS

Books by Eliza Watson   vii

Acknowledgments   xi

Introduction   1

How It All Began: Becoming a Genealogist   4

1. Just Because It's Set in Stone Doesn't Make It True   7

2. Helpful Online Resources   9

3. The Importance of Being Earnest:
   What's in a Name?   11

4. A Newspaper's Gossip Column Might Provide
   Some Juicy Family Details   13

5. A Bit of Neighborly Advice:
   Get to Know Your Ancestors' Neighbors   16

6. City Directories:
   Pointing You in the Right Direction   18

7. United States Naturalization Records   21

8. The Creative Things I've Done to Research
   My Ancestors   24

9. Can't Find Your Ancestors? Get Off-Line!   26

10. Yea or Nay for Ancestry-DNA?   28

11. Playing a Genealogist Supersleuth:
    Inspector Clouseau or Sherlock Holmes?   31

12. Middle-Name Syndrome:
    Don't Ignore These Important Names   33

13. Become a Cemetery Whisperer   36

14. How to Make a Brick Wall Come Tumbling Down   39

15. You Have a DNA Match . . . Now What?   42

16. Your Ancestors Were Divorced? Lucky You!   45

17. Ship Passenger Lists:
    Helping You Embark on Genealogical Research   48

18. Mapping Out Your Ancestors   51

19. How One Clue Helped Me Solve a Ten-Year   54
Family Mystery

20. A Tea Towel Can Help Determine Your   56
Ancestors' Origins

21. Give It the Old College Try: 58
How a School Yearbook Helped Me Solve a Thirty-Year Family Mystery

22. County Directories: 60
Finding Rural Ancestors

23. Connecting the Family Dots: 62
How Linking Clues Can Lead to Answers

24. He's No Joe Blow: 65
The Importance of Sponsors and Witnesses

25. Wills & Probate: 69
Insight into Families, Finances, and Feuds

26. The Social Security Death Index Tells about   71
a Person's Life

27. Ten Ways to Determine Death Dates   74

28. Was She Mary, Molly, or Polly?   78
Identifying Unusual Nicknames

29. Tracing Your Ancestors via Their Occupations   81

30. Don't Forget about the Little Guys: 85
Utilizing Local Libraries and Genealogical Societies for Research

31. Walking among the Dead: 89
What a Cemetery Can Tell You about Your Ancestors' Lives

32. Go Straight to the Source: 94
Questions to Ask Your Relatives

33. Once Upon a Time. . .   99
Writing a Captivating Family Biography

34. Photos Help You Picture Your Family's History   103

35. GEDmatch.com: 107
Connecting with Serious DNA Researchers

36. Military Records: 113
Insight into Your Ancestor's Life and Role in Historical Events

37. Inquiring Minds Want to Know: Author Q&A   118

38. Eliza Watson or MacWattie?   123
Tracing Ancestors with Surname Variations, Changes, and Aliases

39. Family Reunions: 128
   More than Potluck and Playing Cards

40. Truth or Dare: 131
   Are You Prepared for Your DNA Results?

41. How to Make the Most of an Ancestry.com   133
   Account

42. Hello, Is Anyone Out There?   137
   How to Receive Responses from DNA or Family Tree Matches

43. Ten Things I Wish I Had Done Differently   141

44. Ten Assumptions that Can Lead to Creating Your   146
   Own Brick Walls

45. A Genealogy Support Network: 152
   Just What the Doctor Ordered

46. A Game of True or False: 154
   Genealogy Fact or Myth?

47. Researching Your Irish Ancestors   158

48. Tracing Your Family Backward and Then Forward   168
   to Find Living Relatives

49. Walking in Your Ancestors' Footsteps: 172
   Finding Their Family Homesteads

50. I've Done Everything Possible but Still Can't Trace   178
   My Family Line . . .
   Have You Climbed Mount Everest?

My Journey from Southwest Wisconsin, USA, to   185
County Westmeath, Ireland
Coffey Family Case Study

From Type B Blood to Blue Blood: How a Paternal   207
DNA Test Changed My Lineage
Watson Family Case Study

My Ancestors' Cameo Appearances in My Novels   222

Glossary   225

Websites   229

Author's Note   236

About Eliza Watson   237

BOOKS BY ELIZA WATSON

NONFICTION

Genealogy Tips & Quips

FICTION

A MAGS AND BIDDY GENEALOGY MYSTERY SERIES

How to Fake an Irish Wake (Book 1)

How to Snare a Dodgy Heir (Book 2)

How to Handle an Ancestry Scandal (Book 3)

How to Spot a Murder Plot (Book 4)

How to Trace a Cold Case (Book 5)

THE TRAVEL MISHAPS OF CAITY SHAW SERIES

Flying by the Seat of My Knickers (Book 1)

Up the Seine Without a Paddle (Book 2)

My Christmas Goose Is Almost Cooked (Book 3)

My Wanderlust Bites the Dust (Book 4)

Live to Fly Another Day (Book 5)

When in Doubt Don't Chicken Out (Book 6)

FOR ADDITIONAL BOOKS BY ELIZA WATSON VISIT

www.elizawatson.com.

To Jane Daly—a brilliant genealogist and mentor.
Without your assistance, I'd still be wandering through Ireland's
cemeteries searching for ancestry clues.
Thanks a mil!

ACKNOWLEDGMENTS

Genealogy Tips & Quips would never have been written if it weren't for my courageous Irish and Scottish ancestors who immigrated to America and Canada. My longing to discover their untold stories became a major turning point in my life, leading me to their homeland and down an unexpected path. I'm grateful to my parents, Doug and Judy Watson (née Flannery), for sharing my interest in our family heritage. I will forever cherish the memories of our journeys to Ireland and Scotland. Thank you to my living Irish rellies and friends for making all my visits so memorable: Charlotte, Peter, Alexander, and Ivan Molloy; Bernard and Nuala Bolger; Patrick, Geraldine, and Alison Flannery; Joyce, William, and Patricia Fullerton; and Des, Mags, and Darragh Carter.

Thanks to my husband, Mark, and all my friends and family for believing in this project. And also for understanding my obsession, er, passion for genealogy. Nikki Ford and Judy Watson for your in-depth feedback. To beta readers Lori Lynch, Aileen O'Connell, Kyleigh Twaroski, Sandra Watson, and Penny Wolberg. To my brilliant editor, Dori Harrell. Thanks for always going above and beyond. Thanks to you ladies, I was able to publish this book with confidence.

And to the many ancestors I have yet to find. Don't worry—one day I will choose the correct path that leads to you. When I do, you will never be forgotten.

INTRODUCTION

I have fond childhood memories of spending Christmastime with relatives in my parents' hometown in southwestern Wisconsin. A houseful of my mom's relations would gather at my grandma Flannery's or my aunt Susie's. The men would catch up over a beer and a game of Euchre while the women enjoyed coffee and desserts. Everyone was too busy to notice us kids sneaking sodas and homemade holiday treats. On a sugar high, my cousins and I would run around playing until we were forced to snuggle into our sleeping bags on the living room floor and rest up for the next day's activities. I was always sad to leave, knowing we wouldn't make the three-hour journey back to Grandma's until summer, when we often attended large family reunions. The perfect opportunity to sit and chat with my elderly relatives—born in the late 1800s—about our family history and folklore. Oh, how I wish I had. If only I could go back in time . . .

My mom comes from a large, close-knit Irish family, yet little family history was passed down. Thankfully, a few embellished stories about our immigrant ancestors have held on through the generations, which I'll share later. My dad, an only child, had numerous relatives on his mother's Norwegian side, but the only Watson he'd known was his father. My grandpa Watson had no family history knowledge, having been estranged from his father at a young age. When I began researching the Watsons, all I knew was my great-grandpa James Watson had supposedly been a steamfitter in Chicago. Our surname sounded English, like the famous Sherlock Holmes and Watson, so I'd assumed my research would lead to England. In 2007 on my first trip to Ireland with my parents, we'd had no idea my dad had Irish ancestry, as well as Scottish, but very little English.

Since that trip, I've researched more than twenty-five of my maternal and paternal Irish lines, along with several Scottish ones. I've also assisted dozens of friends and family members with ancestry research in Austria, Canada, England, Germany, Hungary, and the US. Besides conducting online research, I have visited numerous historical archives, traipsed through hundreds of cemeteries (many now situated in sheep-filled fields), and located several family homesteads.

I'm not a professional genealogist. I merely play one via the fictional characters in my books. I'm fortunate to be able to combine my two greatest passions—writing and genealogy. In 2016 I began writing a women's fiction series, The Travel Mishaps of Caity Shaw, inspired by my travels as an event planner. A genealogy mystery threaded through the series grew stronger with each book. I enjoyed the genealogy aspect so much that in 2018 I began sharing my research experiences in my author newsletter. Readers often reached out to thank me for the tips and to share their own family research adventures. This bolstered my enthusiasm, and before long I was writing tips faster than I was publishing newsletters. I compiled the tips into this book with the hope of helping others with their ancestry research.

I've included twenty-five tips from my newsletters and twenty-five new tips. The tips are presented in the order they were written to demonstrate the evolution of my research over the two-year period.

Additionally, I've written a Watson case study about a recent paternal DNA test revealing my family's royal lineage and my quest to uncover family secrets. I also compiled a study on tracing my most difficult family line, the Coffeys, over a four-year period. At the back, my family trees provide an at-a-glance view of those ancestors discussed throughout the book, and there is a glossary with genealogical terms. In addition to tips, you'll find a few quips. Besides perseverance, a sense of humor is a necessary trait for a successful genealogist.

So whether you've just begun dabbling in your family history or you have been beating your head against a brick wall for years, I hope you'll find this book insightful, inspirational, and enjoyable. That a tip will give you a new look at an old document and lead you down a path to your ancestor waiting at the end to celebrate the journey with you.

Some family trees have beautiful leaves, and some have just a bunch of nuts. Remember, it is the nuts that make the tree worth shaking. ~Unknown

Eliza

HOW IT ALL BEGAN:
BECOMING A GENEALOGIST

While growing up, I celebrated my Irish heritage on St. Patrick's Day by wearing green along with a pin that read, "The Luck of the Irish." Yet the only family history we knew was that my mother's Flannerys had emigrated from Castlebar, County Mayo, and her Dalys from Kilbeggan, County Westmeath. In 2007, having always wanted to visit Ireland, my parents and I took our first trip to the Emerald Isle. Little did I realize that we weren't merely embarking on a journey to our ancestors' homeland but on a journey that would change my life forever.

After landing at Shannon Airport in western Ireland, we drove up to Castlebar to visit our Flannerys' hometown. We spent hours traipsing through the cemetery and transcribing Flannery graves, unsure if they were related. While walking through Castlebar in my ancestors' footsteps, I knew straight off the trip was going to be an emotional experience.

Over the next few days, we drove down to southwestern Ireland and hit all the main tourist attractions before making our way up to Kilbeggan, which is located in the Midlands. Our ancestor Patrick Daly's 1935 obituary confirmed that his brother Michael had been living in Kilbeggan at the time of Patrick's death. The first stop was at the cemetery to search for Michael's grave. I can recall that breathtaking moment standing in front of an Irish relative's grave for the first time. The same reaction most tourists have while standing on the Cliffs of Moher, staring out at the Atlantic. Not only did Michael Daly's tombstone memorialize him and his wife but also his two daughters. (I'd later learn these daughters were buried with their parents because one had been single and the other abandoned by her husband.) At that moment I said, "Wouldn't it be great to return to Ireland and visit *living* relatives?" And so the genealogical research began.

The Westmeath Genealogy Centre in nearby Moate located baptismal records for Patrick and Michael Daly, their parents' marriage record, and baptismal records for their mother's brothers. Another awe-inspiring moment, obtaining the first of thousands of historical documents for ancestors. Yet the most helpful clues we came away with that trip were the names of Michael Daly's daughters from the tombstone.

In 2007 online records and genealogy how-to books were scarce, so I hired a genealogist in Ireland. (You can find a professional genealogist at Accredited Genealogists Ireland, www.accreditedgenealogists.ie. For other locations, see Association of Professional Genealogists, www.apgen.org/cpages/home.) I selected genealogist Jane Daly, hoping that our shared family surname was a positive sign and that she was possibly related. I'd had no clue that Daly was one of the top twenty most popular Irish surnames. We ended up not being related, but she assisted me with researching numerous family lines, and we became great friends. She located a 1960 newspaper article about Michael Daly's daughter Emily having been struck and killed by a truck. The article noted Emily had three sisters. Even though the two married sisters were identified by their husbands' names—that is, Mrs. D. Swan—a quote given by D. Swan included his first name and where he lived. Bingo. I was off to County Carlow to conduct further research, on my computer anyway.

Through some supersleuthing, I learned which Daly daughter Mr. Swan had married and the names of their children. With the help of Google, I found a descendant who belonged to the Lions Club. A board member was instrumental in connecting me with my first living relative in Ireland. Writing a letter to my newfound relation and receiving her response was priceless. I've since located several Daly relatives and have shared many holidays and memories with a close cousin. I've also connected with Coffey relatives and a Flannery relative, who took me on a tour of our ancestors' *actual* graves in the Castlebar cemetery—a few of which I'd taken pictures of on our first trip in 2007.

The Daly line has turned out to be the easiest one I've researched. If it had been as difficult as my Coffey and Watson lines, I might not have had the perseverance to continue researching more than twenty-five maternal and paternal Irish lines and several Scottish ones. I never dreamed when I embarked on my adventure it would lead to me becoming a genealogist, meeting dozens of Irish relations, writing two fiction series set in Ireland, and buying a renovated 1887 schoolhouse in my Coffey ancestors' hometown. Several of our Coffey, Lynch, and Flanagan relations attended school at our home. A twelve-day trip to Ireland turned out to be the most significant turning point in my life.

Michael Daly's grave in Kilbeggan, County Westmeath, Ireland

1

JUST BECAUSE IT'S SET IN STONE DOESN'T MAKE IT TRUE

When I started researching my Coffey family tree, the only details I knew about my ancestor who emigrated from Ireland to the US were his birth and death dates obtained from his gravestone. The birth year was incorrect. The Irish rarely celebrated birthdays and often didn't know their birth years. If a gravestone states an ancestor was born in 1825, and you discover a potential baptismal certificate from 1822, don't immediately assume it's not your relative's. I've also found misspelled names and incorrect maiden names on tombstones.

A different mother's name was noted on three Watson siblings' US death certificates. None were correct. Fortunately, I had their Canadian baptismal certificates with their mother's right name. She died when her children were young, so their spouses and kids may not have recalled, or ever known, her name.

Beware of inaccurate online family trees. People often click on Ancestry.com's green "hint" leaf and add a *possible* relative to their tree without verifying the information. I once found a tree with a father born *after* his son and a couple married a century *after* the woman had died.

My ancestor Margaret Coffey's obituary stated that her family lived in Maryland Heights, Maryland, after emigrating from Ireland. I searched Maryland's genealogical documents before I happened upon the fact that *Maryland* Heights is located in Missouri. Who'd have thought?

In the US Census, I have found Coffey spelled as Caffey, Caffrey, and Claffey. Always use the "Sounds Like" or "Soundex" option on search sites. The Soundex is a phonetic index that groups together names that sound alike but are spelled differently—for example, Cook and Koch. Enumerators—census takers—often couldn't understand the plethora of ethnic accents, and people couldn't spell their own last names. Also remember that people often didn't know their birth years or didn't have the math skills to correctly determine their ages. Little Jimmy might have been three years old in the 1870 census and only seven in 1880.

I've learned the hard way that it's critical to at least attempt to obtain genealogical information from three sources before I consider it accurate.

2

HELPFUL ONLINE RESOURCES

You can't turn on the TV without seeing an Ancestry.com, www.ancestry.com, commercial. If you are just starting to dabble in research, they offer a free fourteen-day trial. A great non-subscription alternative is FamilySearch at www.familysearch.org. Ancestry.com offers more than 20 billion historical records. FamilySearch offers over 7 billion searchable records, but also 3 billion images that haven't yet been indexed. I often use one site in conjunction with the other. For example, I was unable to locate a family in England's 1891 census because their surname had been transcribed incorrectly on Ancestry.com. I was about to give up, when I found the family in the same census on the FamilySearch site. I have encountered this numerous times on various sites, so if you are unable to locate a record, check another resource.

A gravestone may provide a gold mine of information, including a spouse's name, death date, birth date, country of origin, and more. What if you can't fly off to another country to traipse through cemeteries? Two great international sites are Find a Grave, www.findagrave.com, and BillionGraves, www.billiongraves.com. These also often provide gravestone photos, memorials, known children, and possible family members buried in the same vicinity. BillionGraves has GPS locations to guide you directly to the gravesite, which is helpful in larger cemeteries. The information on both websites is provided by volunteers, and millions of new records are added annually.

If you can't find a grave online, find a local volunteer to assist at Random Acts of Genealogical Kindness, www.raogk.org. I've had volunteers around the world searching through cemeteries for graves, local newspapers for obituaries, and courthouse records for birth, marriage, or death certificates. The volunteers charge for expenses but not for their time.

Besides state and local historical and genealogical organizations, don't forget the local libraries. They will often assist with finding obituaries or other information in old newspapers. They may even have a genealogy page with an obituary index or histories of families from the area. If it's not noted on their website, call and ask. They'll likely be happy to help.

Collaborate with others researching your family surnames on forums. A lot of local historians also hang out on these sites and will volunteer to assist. A few of my favorites are www.genealogy.com/forum, www.ancestry.com/boards, and www.familytreeforum.com.

Two of my top sites for researching my Irish family history are www.rootsireland.ie and www.census.nationalarchives.ie.

Google your ancestor's name and any known details. Get creative. I've traced trees forward searching for possible living relatives in Ireland. As I mentioned, I found a relation noted on a Lions Club website. I contacted a board member, and he put me in touch with the man, who turned out to be the missing link needed to trace the family line. In appreciation, I sent them all sweatshirts from the Wisconsin Lions Club. Also, you might search a name on Google and, voilà, up pops your family tree created by an unknown rellie. I've only been this lucky once, around St. Paddy's Day, so maybe it was the luck of the Irish at work.

3

THE IMPORTANCE OF BEING EARNEST:

WHAT'S IN A NAME?

Like dates, names can also lead you down the right or wrong paths in genealogical research. I was two years into my Irish ancestry research when I stumbled upon an important discovery that helped me break through a brick wall and locate my Coffey family in Ireland.

The Irish traditionally adhered to a family naming pattern until the early 1900s. The first son was named after the father's father. The second son after the mother's father. The third son after the father. The fourth son after the father's oldest brother. The fifth son after the father's second oldest brother, and so on down the line through fifteen kids. The daughters were named in the same pattern after the maternal side of the family. It's critical to know where in order each child was born, both living and dead. When a child died, his or her name was often used again for the next-born son or daughter. This demonstrates just how important it was to pass down family names and how confusing it can get for genealogists.

Knowing my Patrick Coffey's children's names and ages provided me with his parents' and brothers' names, enabling me to search Ireland's records and cemeteries to eventually locate his family. Even though Patrick, James, and John were common Irish names, I could rule out other Coffey clans with names such as Hugh, William, and Matthew.

The naming pattern isn't an exact science. If the pattern resulted in a duplication of names, such as both grandfathers having had the same name, then the parents skipped to the next name on the list. Personal reasons also came into play. A mother might not have wanted to name a child after her abusive father.

It can become a game of mental gymnastics, putting together the pieces of the naming puzzle. However, it can be critical in tracing your family tree. Luckily, my Coffeys strictly adhered to the naming pattern, or I'd never have found my family in Ireland. Even if the pattern was loosely followed, names had personal meanings and weren't randomly selected as they often are today. You just have to determine what role the names played in the family.

While transcribing five weathered Coffey tombstones in an Irish cemetery, I saw the family naming pattern put into practice going back five generations. Each stone memorialized numerous family members, including several maiden names and a few unknown names.

The Scottish and British followed the same or a similar naming pattern as the Irish. Many nationalities adhered to family naming patterns. Did yours?

4

A NEWSPAPER'S GOSSIP COLUMN
MIGHT PROVIDE SOME JUICY
FAMILY DETAILS

Another breakthrough with my Coffey family came from my ancestor Margaret Coffey's obituary, which noted two women and their husbands from Iowa having attended the funeral. I located the couples' marriage records online and discovered the women's father's name was Michael Coffey. But how was Michael related to my ancestor Patrick Coffey? A brother, cousin, nephew, or coincidence?

I went to the Wisconsin Historical Society and obtained twenty-five rolls of microfilm for the local newspapers from that time period. I scrolled through the gossip columns until I came across a snippet about the Coffey boys traveling to Iowa to visit their "uncle" Michael. Yet knowing that newspapers sometimes printed incorrect information, I searched until I found another notice referencing their "uncle." Bingo.

If I hadn't found Margaret's obituary, the newspaper's gossip column would have been a great resource. It often mentioned people in town not only visiting the living but also those attending funerals. The column would include residents involved in accidents or those affected by epidemics and illnesses. It would also pay condolences to parents who'd lost a newborn or young child, helping you identify unknown family members.

On a happier note, engagement announcements provided married surnames for those hard-to-trace female ancestors. Also, well-wishes to someone relocating to another town or state for a new job helps genealogists track them down. If people hadn't heard the latest news through the grapevine, they could read about it in the weekly gossip column. While I was growing up, our local paper had a gossip column until the early 1980s.

The *Boston Pilot* had an interesting personal column titled "Missing Friends." From October 1831 to October 1921, the newspaper printed almost forty-five thousand advertisements from people searching for lost friends and relatives who had emigrated from Ireland to the United States. These ads provided details of the missing emigrant's life, including the county and parish of the person's birth, when he left Ireland, the port of arrival in North America, family members' names, and more. These advertisements have been compiled into several volumes of books and can be found on Ancestry.com and Findmypast, www.findmypast.com. I could spend all day perusing these ads.

Here is an ad placed in 1847 by a person searching for a Flannery couple from Derreenmanus, County Mayo, homeland of my Flannerys. I haven't confirmed a connection, even though Richard was a family name, but I sure hope these relations found each other. You can often feel a person's sense of desperation to locate loved ones. This ad provides a lot of genealogical information. However, I've come across ones that have even more details, such as a physical description, enabling you to picture your ancestor.

Of RICHARD FLANNERY, and ELLEN, his wife, formerly of Derreenmanus, near Castlebar, Co. Mayo. When last heard from they were in Constableville, NY. Any information respecting them will be thankfully received by her brother and

*his brother-in-law, Patrick McDonnell, addressed to him in
care of Mr. Peter Carney, Brookline, MA.*

You can search numerous online newspapers at Ancestry.com
and www.newspapers.com. The Irish Genealogy Toolkit website
provides information for Irish papers at www.irish-genealogy-toolkit.
com/irish-newspaper-archives.html.

The following are two websites on using newspapers in your
research and how to find articles online:

www.theancestorhunt.com/blog/the-5-best-free-sites-for-online-
newspaper-research-for-genealogy

www.genealogybank.com/explore/newspapers/all

5

A BIT OF NEIGHBORLY ADVICE:

GET TO KNOW YOUR
ANCESTORS' NEIGHBORS

A population census helped me trace my Watsons by their occupation—steamfitters—an uncommon profession in Chicago before the Great Fire in 1871. I discovered via a census that my ancestor had ten children, but only eight were still living at that time. I found the birth certificates for the two unknown children, which helped me fill in the family naming pattern. (See Tip 3 for details on the naming pattern.) Depending on the country, the census may also provide a person's immigration year, religion, birthplace, marital status, and much more.

So once you've found your ancestor's record, your census research is done, right? Wrong. That is merely a tidbit of the information the census provides. Look beyond the family's transcribed record and also at the original document. Not only to ensure that all the information was transcribed correctly but to see who lived next door to, or near, the family. This often provides more valuable insight and clues than the family themselves.

A steamfitter with the last name Turney lived next door to my Watsons. Curious that he had the same occupation as my family, I did a bit of research and discovered that the two families were in business together. The man was Elizabeth Watson's brother. (It's purely a coincidence that I was named after my second-great-grandmother.) Learning that her maiden name was Turney enabled me to piece together Elizabeth's family and trace them back to Canada. I have found missing family members—presumed dead or having relocated —living a few doors down from ancestors, caring for a widowed aunt or an elderly grandmother. These discoveries helped me to further trace the family trees.

People often immigrated to a specific area of a country because a friend or relative from their homeland now lived there. So if your ancestor lived in a rural or urban setting, it's likely that they had a deeper connection to their neighbors than sharing the same zip code. I'll further discuss this topic in my next tip on city directories.

6

CITY DIRECTORIES:

POINTING YOU IN THE RIGHT DIRECTION

The first ancestors I researched lived in small rural communities. It wasn't until I began researching my Watsons in Chicago that I discovered city directories. Prior to the telephone book, there was the city directory that listed a head-of-household name, address, profession, and in some cases ethnicity. Not only did the directory provide more information than the later telephone book, but you didn't have to have a phone to be listed in one. Chicago directories span from 1839 to 1928, having been first published two years after the city was incorporated with a population of 4,000. London's first directory dates back to 1588, and Philadelphia has the honor of having published the first directory in the US in 1785. Keep in mind that not all residents were included in the directory since some directories charged a fee, but most people wanted to be located.

The information included in directories varies by city. Most include front matter with information about government, civic, and religious organizations, an alphabetical residential section, which primarily lists heads of households, and a back section that lists businesses by specialty. An added bonus, the 1871 Chicago directory listed a person's country of origin. I have probably used city directories more than any other resource in my genealogical research.

These annual directories help track the movement of people between the release of US Census records every ten years. When I discovered that the 1890 census had been mostly destroyed in a 1921 fire at the Commerce Department in Washington, DC, I turned to the city directories to help fill in that twenty-year gap between the 1880 census and the 1900 census. My Watsons first appeared in a Chicago city directory in the mid-1860s, enabling me to pinpoint when the family emigrated from Ontario, Canada, to Chicago. I stopped searching for them in the Canadian census and found them in the US one. Their home addresses allowed me to map out all the Watsons in Chicago, which was a small number at that time. (Mapping out addresses entailed first converting Chicago's pre-1909 street numbers and names to the updated ones.) I discovered those who lived in close proximity to each other were often related.

The directories also noted occupations. In addition to his home address, James Watson listed his company, James Watson & Son Steam Heating Apparatus, in the residential listing. Learning that my Watsons had an entrepreneurial spirit was an interesting find. A steamfitter was a niche profession, so I scanned the directory for others with that same one. I found a Charles Watson and several men with surnames linked to my Watsons. I am still trying to fit them all into the family tree.

I utilized the Montreal, Canada, city directory to research my Connolly family—Bridget Connolly married James Watson in 1841. In the 1842 directory, there were only five Connolly/Conley families listed. I found two of these families living next to the military barracks where James Watson lived. Hmm . . . I am using the directory in conjunction with the Notre Dame Catholic Church records to hopefully determine Bridget Connolly's family. Fingers crossed.

In Kingston, Ontario, I discovered that a potential MaGee relation had what turned out to be two brothers living just down the street from James Watson. When one of them disappeared from the directory the following year, his widow was listed. This helped me narrow down his death date and locate his obituary.

In desperation—and believe me, I've been desperate—I've taken an ancestor's address and gone through an entire city directory to find people living with them or next door. Yes, that was time consuming, but like I always say, even more than an Ancestry.com subscription and luck, it takes perseverance to piece together your family tree!

Ancestry.com and Fold3, www.fold3.com, are subscription sites that offer a large collection of city directories. Fold3 allows you to search the digitized pages for specific surnames, addresses, and keywords. The following websites offer free access to many directories:

www.familysearch.org
www.archive.org
www.books.google.com

7

UNITED STATES
NATURALIZATION RECORDS

I had been researching my Irish ancestors for several years before I discovered the importance of naturalization papers. I visited a historical records depository in Wisconsin and searched through thousands of delicate tissue-paper sheets before discovering my relative Patrick Coffey's Declaration of Intention filed in 1852. His paper noted his birth county in Ireland, his age, his arrival date, and his port location. This helped me narrow down his possible home counties in Ireland from thirty-two to one. Researching a smaller area makes much more efficient use of your time.

In general, US naturalization was a two-step process that took five years for a person to become a legal citizen. A person had to live in the US for two years to file a Declaration of Intention, renouncing his allegiance to foreign governments. After three additional years, the person could file a Petition for Naturalization. The duration of this process changed several times and varied widely. For example, Patrick Coffey filed his Declaration of Intention only ten months, not two years, after arriving in America. The information provided also varied widely. The papers filed by my ancestors in the counties surrounding Patrick's had no genealogical details.

There is also no consistency in where people filed for naturalization or where the records are now stored. Prior to 1906, naturalization papers could be filed with a municipal, county, state, or federal court. Some naturalization papers are online at sites such as Ancestry.com and FamilySearch. Their databases contain images of original records from US district and circuit courts. If the naturalization records are held on a local level, you may need to provide a courthouse clerk with at least a general idea of when your ancestor became a citizen. Also keep in mind that your ancestor may have filed the Declaration of Intention in one court and state and filed the Petition for Naturalization several years later in another court and state. Many people lived near their port of arrival for a few years before settling elsewhere in the country.

The 1900–1930 censuses list a person's immigration year and if a man was a naturalized citizen. The 1920 census notes the actual year of naturalization. If your ancestor died before the 1900 census, how do you estimate his naturalization year? If he had a living male relative in 1900, check his census record. Family members often immigrated together. Men generally applied for citizenship as soon as possible to obtain the right to vote and to apply for homestead land. However, it's estimated that 25 percent of immigrants didn't become citizens. (Women and children were automatically citizens when the man of the family became one.)

Researching pre-1900 censuses can help you narrow down when a person first appeared in America. Also check out voter registration lists, which often note naturalization dates. Trying to find your ancestor's arrival date on a ship manifest can prove difficult. Prior to Ellis Island opening in 1892 in New York City, most manifests only included a person's name—often barely legible—age, occupation, and country of origin. Once Ellis Island opened, arrival records provided a person's hometown, country, the name of a relative living there, and often the name and address of the person the immigrant planned to live with in the US. I would still obtain the person's naturalization record if possible, since it likely provides more personal details.

I've merely scratched the surface on naturalization records. You can get in-depth information at the following sites:

www.libertyellisfoundation.org/passenger

www.naturalizationrecords.com

www.familysearch.org/
wiki/en/United_States_Naturalization_and_Citizenship

www.archives.gov/research/naturalization

8

THE CREATIVE THINGS I'VE DONE TO RESEARCH MY ANCESTORS

I visited a courthouse in southern Wisconsin to research ancestor records. There on a shelf next to the marriage index binder was a jail log from 1880 to 1910, which was discovered when the old jail was torn down. I searched the records hoping one of my ancestors had been incarcerated—for a minor offense. A man with the last name Coffey had spent the night in jail for drunkenness. Although he lived just over the border in Illinois, I was curious if he'd been there visiting my ancestors—the only Coffey family in that area. I researched the man but haven't yet found a connection. I still believe there is one. Look beyond your typical genealogy documents when visiting a courthouse, library, or historical center. You never know what you might find in jail logs, school admission records, area business directories, church newsletters, or county fair programs.

When tracing ancestors' lines forward searching for living relatives, I've sent letters to people around the world. Many mailing addresses can be located online with a little research. I've also reached out to people on social media sites, such as Facebook. In Ireland I once even left a note with my contact information inside a plastic baggie on a grave that had fresh flowers, assuming there was still family in the area. I never received a response, but it was worth a shot.

Every record and document I have for my ancestor James Watson note that he was from Scotland. But what if he wasn't *born* in Scotland? After hiring a researcher to check church records in Glasgow, I came up empty. For the heck of it, while perusing an Irish records site one night, I put in my ancestor's name. I found a baptismal record for a James Watson born in 1811 to John and Barbara Watson. My James's birth year and his mother's name. I wondered if his father's name, James, could have been documented or transcribed incorrectly. Then I recalled that a city directory later listed James Jr. as John. Maybe the men preferred the nickname John to the more formal name James. I'm going to have someone review the original document. I'm not letting a minor detail, such as a different first name, stop me. Also, John Watson was a soldier in the Donegal Regiment, part of Her Majesty's Military. Being in the British armed forces meant he could quite possibly have been Scottish.

Tracing your ancestry requires you to be creative and assertive. I once stopped at a nursing home in Ireland to visit with locals about the area in the 1940s. I've gone into pubs, restaurants, and post offices searching for relations and local historians, which has led to me knocking on dozens of strangers' doors. Several times I've knocked on the *wrong* doors, but people are typically more than happy to point you in the right direction. After all, you'll likely head down a lot of wrong paths before finding the right one.

9

CAN'T FIND YOUR ANCESTORS? GET OFF-LINE!

Many genealogists estimate that only 10 percent of ancestry records are available online. I have found about a quarter of my family records via the web. In 2007 when I began researching, I hired genealogists to locate documents in archives and churches. Many of those documents are now available on the internet. However, some records will never be online due to privacy laws, cost, and remote locations.

When a friend declared she was done researching her family line because she'd spent months on Ancestry.com without any success, I gave her a pep talk. Despite often wanting to admit defeat myself, I assured her that online research is merely scratching the surface. That her ancestors' information is out there waiting to be discovered.

Many states don't have civil birth, death, or marriage records online. Wisconsin law required counties to register deaths starting in 1852. The Wisconsin Historical Society has an online death index for pre-1907 records, most of which date from 1880 when the law started being strictly enforced. A record can be ordered for a fee. The lack of early civil records makes church records critical. However, I'm rarely successful in obtaining these records in the US despite making donations and having a cousin who is a nun with connections to the

Catholic church. Priests often consider parish records confidential, even if the person was your direct relative and has been deceased for a hundred years. If your ancestor lived in a major city, you might find church records online, depending on the denomination. I highly recommend finding a way to obtain these records, be it visiting the church or reaching out to a local historian or parishioner for assistance. The records provide important family information, such as the names of witnesses and sponsors.

The lack of online records forced me to visit the Wisconsin Historical Society, ranked one of the top five historical societies in the US, with the second-largest newspaper collection. I spent days searching their archives and scanning hundreds of newspapers for obituaries, gossip columns, ads, and other information. While chatting with the librarian, he suggested I check the Galena, Illinois, newspaper since that would have been the main market center for southwestern Wisconsin. Good to know. Librarians, local historians, and genealogists are often your best resource.

If your ancestors lived within driving distance of you, take a road trip there so you can visit the courthouse, records depository, historical societies, cemeteries, and churches. Besides finding information you are looking for, you might stumble upon many resources you never knew existed. If you're unable to visit the location, local genealogical or historical societies often have volunteers. I've previously mentioned connecting with many volunteers and local historians through Random Acts of Genealogical Kindness and also via forums.

10

YEA OR NAY FOR ANCESTRY-DNA?

I'd been researching my Watson family tree for seven years when I joined my parents and sister on a visit to our ancestor's homeland, Scotland. Prior to the trip, my goal was to locate living relatives to visit. James Watson's military papers noted he was from Pollokshaws, outside Glasgow. Watson turned out to be a common surname in the Glasgow area, and the number of historical records was overwhelming. I'm an old-school genealogist. I love spending hours searching through courthouse and church records. However, time was of the essence, so I took what I thought would be the easy way out and turned to DNA testing.

At the end of 2017, my dad took a DNA test that resulted in a few hundred matches, which has now grown to thousands. Most connections were distant cousins. Many were related to him through his mother's Norwegian line. I reached out to several matches with undisclosed ethnicities and didn't receive one response. I decided that many people take this test merely to learn their ethnic origins and that they are not interested in researching their family trees.

I uploaded my dad's DNA results to GEDmatch, www.gedmatch.com—a free third-party genealogy website that allows you to load your test data from AncestryDNA, www.ancestry.com/dna; MyHeritage, www.myheritage.com; 23andMe, www.23andme.com; or FamilyTreeDNA, www.familytreedna.com. It enables you to compare DNA matches from all the major testing companies. (GEDmatch will be discussed in detail in Tip 35.) I assumed if people took the extra step to join GEDmatch, they were likely more serious about genealogical research. My dad ended up with thousands of matches. His closest connections' most recent shared ancestors went back four generations. Within days a woman contacted me that her grandma Watson was from Scotland. But my excitement was short lived. Despite extensive research on both our ends, we never determined our families' connection. I haven't yet come across others with the surname Watson in their trees. However, several matches have the surname MaGee, which isn't even a known family name but keeps popping up. Interesting . . .

To weed out people related through my dad's maternal line, I had him take a Y-DNA paternal test. This test can only be taken by a male in the family. A male's Y chromosome is passed down from father to son virtually unchanged for thousands of years. A Y-DNA test is the most expensive one I've had a relative take—it costs $250—whereas I've purchased an autosomal test, which tests chromosomes inherited from both parents, at Ancestry.com for as low as $59.99. Father's Day, Mother's Day, and Christmas are all popular times for DNA test promotions. I haven't had a relative take the mtDNA test —testing only the maternal line—which appears to run around $150. The Y-DNA test resulted in only thirty-eight male matches. There were a wide variety of surnames, including numerous Burkes, but not one Watson. I assumed the matches' last names went back before the use of standardized surnames. I didn't know where to begin trying to determine their connection. (Update: in Tip 35, I discuss how I later realized this paternal test was providing clues I didn't fully comprehend at the time I wrote this tip.) I then discovered that GEDmatch wouldn't allow me to upload paternal test results, only results from an autosomal test.

Even though I didn't locate any Watson relatives in Scotland, we had a great trip. Now, I am impatiently waiting for some closer relatives, hopefully with the surname Watson, to appear as a match on these three sites.

On his paternal side, my father is a third-generation only child without any known living relatives. This is further complicated by the fact that the fourth generation, my dad's great-grandfather, was the only child with offspring, my dad's grandfather. This means I'll be lucky if a third cousin—who shares second-great-grandparents—shows up as a match. It could take several years before the right person takes a DNA test and solves the mystery of my Watson ancestors.

In conclusion, I found both pros and cons to taking a DNA test. Don't expect immediate connections with long-lost relations. Also, know which test best meets your research needs—autosomal, Y-DNA paternal, or an mtDNA maternal test.

11

PLAYING A GENEALOGIST
SUPERSLEUTH:

INSPECTOR CLOUSEAU OR
SHERLOCK HOLMES?

Sometimes I feel more like the bumbling Inspector Clouseau than the skilled Sherlock Holmes when conducting genealogical research. Yet if I spend enough time on Ancestry.com, I'll usually solve my genealogy mystery either by sheer luck or deductive reasoning. The following is an example of how tracing your ancestry line requires keeping an open mind while piecing together clues to solve the puzzle. It can also involve a bit of mental gymnastics, which might require giving this tip a second read.

While researching Richard Tubbs for a friend, I knew he was born circa 1851 in London. I located the Tubbs family in the 1861 and 1871 censuses, which confirmed Richard's approximate birth date, his parents' names—Richard Sr. and Elizabeth—and the family's address.

I searched Ancestry.com for Richard Jr.'s or his younger sister Ann's baptismal or civil birth records, but came up empty. Next I looked for his parents' marriage record. I found a Richard Fossey Tubbs and Elizabeth Hale married in 1857. Six years *after* Richard Jr. was supposedly born and three years *after* his sister's birth. I might have assumed I had the wrong couple. However, the address on the

31

marriage record was next door to where the family had lived in the 1861 census. I now had the critical piece of information that would eventually help me piece together this mysterious family. The father's middle name was Fossey.

I used the father's full name to search for Richard Jr.'s 1851 birth record. I found a baptismal record for a Richard Hale. I recalled that my Richard's mother's maiden name was Hale. The record noted the parents as Elizabeth Hale and Richard "Fossey" Hale. Well, wasn't that interesting? Fossey being an uncommon name, I believed I had the correct family. I put in their daughter's birth year with the last name Hale, and ta-da, a record now appeared for an Ann Jane Hale with parents Richard and Elizabeth. FYI, the children's civil birth records were also filed with the mother's maiden name, Hale.

Next I searched for the family in the 1851 census and found Richard and Betsy "Fossey" living at the same address as the children's baptismal records. Now their *last* name was the father Richard's *middle* name. Over a six-year period, the family used *three* different surnames on church and government documents. The mother's maiden name, Hale. The father's middle name, Fossey, and his last name, Tubbs. Had they been hiding from the law? Perhaps, but I believe it was because the couple had two children born out of wedlock. Despite the family having lived at the same residence when two baptisms and their marriage occurred, these events were held at *three* different churches. A family changing churches (not their religion) while remaining at the same residence was uncommon.

Once the parents were married, all future census and vital records noted family members with the last name Tubbs. However, I have not yet located Richard Tubbs Jr.'s marriage record or his children's baptismal or birth records. Maybe Richard Jr.'s children were born prior to his marriage and he followed family tradition, giving them his wife's maiden name, Wright. And so the mystery continues . . .

MIDDLE-NAME SYNDROME:

DON'T IGNORE THESE IMPORTANT NAMES

I recently read an article in which the author claimed that middle names have little significance when conducting genealogical research. I strongly disagree. I have obtained hundreds of Irish baptismal certificates dated prior to 1900, and not one noted a middle name. After the Irish immigrated to America, many gave their children middle names to memorialize relatives back in their homeland, demonstrating the importance of these names. Besides the fact that a person sometimes goes by his middle name rather than his first name, there are a few other reasons these names have been helpful in my genealogical research.

My third-great-grandfather Patrick Coffey adhered to the Irish family naming pattern after he immigrated to America and had children. Based on the pattern, his third-born son should have been named Patrick, after himself. However, after extensive research I was convinced that the third son was John, named after Patrick's eldest brother. I later discovered a record that documented his son's name as John *Patrick*. If I hadn't learned John's *middle* name was his father's, I might have questioned the accuracy of my research and still be searching for a Patrick Jr. Out of Patrick's five sons, the only other middle name I've learned is Thomas *Lawrence*. While transcribing our Coffey headstones in Ireland, I came across a Lawrence Coffey, my Patrick's uncle.

The paper trail for my ancestor James William Watson in Chicago disappeared after his WWI draft card. I wondered if he'd died in the war. Then I discovered a WWII draft card for a William James Watson with the same birth date. It turned out James had switched his middle and first names after he'd divorced, possibly to elude family obligations. If I hadn't known James's middle name, I never would have checked a document for a William James.

I am helping an elderly English lady trace her ancestry with the hope of learning her grandfather's identity. Her father's name was documented on his birth certificate and in England's 1891 census as Frederick George. The boy's middle name, George, was his maternal grandfather's name. However, the name Frederick was nowhere to be found in his maternal line, so it was likely his father's or paternal grandfather's name. This was a major clue. Frederick's mother might have chosen the name hoping to unite with her child's father. In the 1901 census and all future documents, the boy's name is recorded as George Frederick. The first and middle names were switched. The mother had possibly cut ties with her baby's father and preferred to now call her son by her father's name.

I have found numerous Scottish and English relations with middle names that seemed more like last names. That's because they were family surnames. It was common to use a mother's maiden name or other important family name for middle names. Such as my relation Alice Bonner Housley Malvina Briggs. Wow. That's a mouthful, but a name loaded with clues. It turned out her paternal grandmother was Bridget Housley Bonner. Her great-grandmother was Maria Housley. Her great-grandfather, Ambrose Franklin Bonner. I could make an educated guess that Ambrose's mother's maiden name was Franklin. I didn't have to because I found a document confirming her maiden name was indeed Franklin. So Alice's names went back *four* generations.

What about the first names Alice and Malvina? Maybe I'd have to go back six generations to learn their place in the family tree. If only every ancestor had given each child five names. Yet it also begs the question of why all her names were from her father's side of the family and not one known name from her mother's side. Traditionally, the firstborn daughter would have been named after her maternal side. Maybe the names haven't yet been discovered on the maternal side? Hmm . . . Or does it speak to the parents' relationship? A bit of a controlling husband possibly?

Which historical documents are the best resources for finding middle names? Birth and death records are hit or miss. I have found more middle names on death records than birth records. I have several birth records that don't even have *first* names, which were sometimes decided on later. Yet I have one like Alice Brigg's English birth record that gave her name as Alice Bonner H M Briggs. With the help of other documents, I determined what names the initials stood for.

Censuses and city directories often include middle initials but rarely middle names. Typically naturalization records and military records—such as WWI draft cards—provide middle names. It's not easy to locate the important yet often elusive middle name. Yet what *is* easy about genealogical research?

13

BECOME A CEMETERY
WHISPERER

Family members and I make an annual spring trip to southwestern Wisconsin to decorate our relatives' graves. I've located many of the graves since 2007, when I began conducting genealogical research. At each cemetery I share the history of our ancestors who immigrated to America. My mind wanders to their families' graves in Ireland, which my immigrant relations never returned home to memorialize. Thankfully, I've had the opportunity to do so when visiting Ireland.

I've explored dozens of old Irish cemeteries located in the middle of sheep fields, at monastic ruins, and at abandoned churches. I've traversed some rough terrain and once had my foot slip into a sunken grave. I have found the remotely located cemeteries via Google's satellite map, cemetery groundsmen, and area locals. It was thanks to a cousin putting me in touch with an unrelated Coffey gentleman that I discovered our Coffey graves. The family plot with five weathered headstones is located ten miles from where my ancestor was born and baptized. The tombstones enabled me to trace my Coffey family tree back to the early 1700s—a feat I couldn't have accomplished with Ireland's spotty historical records. The family had apparently originated in that area, then over the years dispersed to surrounding locations.

I haven't been lucky enough to find a family plot for my Dalys from Kilbeggan, County Westmeath. Daly is the twenty-fourth most common surname in Ireland, so researching baptismal certificates has been overwhelming. Peter and Sarah Daly had only two children, making it impossible to utilize the Irish family naming pattern to piece together the tree. However, I assume their firstborn son, Patrick, my second-great-grandfather, was named after his paternal grandfather.

Patrick's brother is buried in Kilbeggan, but I've been unable to locate his parents' grave. They died in 1898 and 1921, so their tombstone is likely not too weathered to read. Like my Coffeys, they might have been buried in an old family plot ten miles from where they'd lived. While in Ireland, I visited a cemetery located just south of Kilbeggan in County Offaly. I found graves for a half dozen Daly families—none of them my Peter and Sarah. I was disappointed, yet the headstones helped me rule out several Peters born to these other families and not mine.

So how will I ever find my Dalys' graves? In the US a person's burial place is usually noted on the death certificate or in an obituary. Death certificates in Ireland, at least pre-1941, don't list burial locations. I haven't found obituaries there dated before 1940, and few Catholic burial records have survived. I've visited genealogical societies and libraries to peruse cemetery transcriptions compiled by local historians. And I've searched online at Find a Grave and Billion-Graves. I will continue traipsing through Ireland's cemeteries until I one day locate them.

Cemetery in Avoca Valley, County Wicklow, Ireland

14

HOW TO MAKE A BRICK WALL COME TUMBLING DOWN

"I've searched everywhere and still come up empty." I often hear this from disheartened researchers, both novices and experts. My response? "Keep looking!" Remember, many genealogists estimate that only 10 percent of historical documents are online—the rest are housed in libraries, church archives, or places yet to be discovered. If you conducted research several years ago, more information is now readily available. And sometimes it's a matter of looking at old information in a new light. Here are several tips for breaking down your genealogy brick walls.

EVEN EXPERTS MAKE MISTAKES

If a professional genealogist or an experienced volunteer comes up empty, consider double-checking his work. I've had several researchers fail to locate historical records that I later found. Deciphering faded and illegible documents can be difficult, and surname spellings were rarely standardized prior to the 1900s. Last year before a family ancestry trip to Ireland and Scotland, my gut told me I was heading down the wrong path and that my ancestors hadn't been married in Ireland. A week before leaving, I rechecked church archives in Canada. Due to time constraints, I was unable to hire a new set of eyes and had to request that the same researcher double-check the records. His second attempt was successful, at no charge. My ancestors' names had been misspelled. I was upset that I didn't have time to pursue this new lead before the trip. Always listen to your instincts.

CONNECT WITH PEOPLE, EVEN IF YOU DON'T BELIEVE THERE'S A FAMILY CONNECTION

My dad volunteers at a veterans' home, where he met a James Watson —the same name as our Scottish ancestor. The man's son—their family historian—didn't believe we were related but reached out to me. I couldn't find a family connection either, but I emailed him my newsletter column's genealogy tips. He wasn't familiar with the Scottish family naming pattern. When he realized that the families in his tree adhered to the pattern, he was inspired to continue his research. Who knows—we might one day confirm a family connection.

REACH OUT TO EXTENDED FAMILY MEMBERS

After learning about my Patrick Coffey's brother, I traced his family forward and located a descendant. She was sweet and apologetic that the *only* thing she knew was the name of the town where he was possibly born. The town matched the one I believed to be Patrick's birthplace, confirming the accuracy of my research.

REVISIT PREVIOUS CONTACTS

I was reviewing old email correspondence from fellow researchers, and one in 2009 jumped out at me. I realized that based on the family naming pattern, we were likely related. I'd previously dismissed a connection because I hadn't been familiar with the naming pattern.

You may have gained more experience or information since your last communication with the person, or maybe he has. Reach out to him.

REVIEW YOUR EARLIER RESEARCH

After reading a magazine article and learning that my Butler ancestors had lived within miles of the actor Gerard Butler's grandparents, I pulled out my Butler family research from several years ago. My sister and I had always thought my nephew looked like the actor. I was dying to know if we were related to him. In merely a day, I found several records online that weren't previously available or that I'd overlooked. I then reviewed the original parish records online and discovered additional family members, enabling me to piece together more of my Butler family tree. I am still hoping to connect the actor to our tree. You never know who might help you break down that brick wall. It might even be a famous celebrity!

15

YOU HAVE A DNA MATCH . . . NOW WHAT?

When I received my mother's DNA test results from Ancestry.com, I immediately searched for those matches with Butlers in their family trees. Besides still wanting to find a connection to the actor Gerard Butler, I hoped to locate my ancestor Eliza Butler's three brothers, who'd disappeared shortly after immigrating to America in 1852. A fourth-cousin DNA match—92 percent Irish—piqued my interest. Here is how I proceeded:

STEP ONE

I printed off a cousinhood chart detailing how to calculate this person's relationship to my mom based on their amount of shared DNA. These charts are available online. I concluded that this person and my mother likely shared third-great-grandparents. My mom's third-great-grandparents were Michael Butler and Elinor Byrne.

STEP TWO

I contacted the match, Mary, who replied within a day and happily shared her family tree. Her mother, a Butler, had emigrated from County Wicklow in the 1900s and was descended from a Thomas Butler born in 1831. The Thomas who'd immigrated to America with my Eliza Butler was born circa 1831. My Thomas's paper trail ended with his Civil War enlistment record. I'd assumed he'd either died in the war or remained in the area where he'd mustered out. Instead, had Thomas returned to Ireland?

STEP THREE

I reviewed Mary's and my mom's shared DNA matches. I contacted all sixteen matches and determined how they were related. Luckily, many of them responded, and knowing their relationships proved helpful. Everything to this point led me to believe I'd found my missing Thomas, except for one thing. Our families shared several similar names, but a few critical ones were missing. Based on the Irish family naming pattern, Mary's ancestor Thomas's parents were John and Hannah, not Michael and Elinor—my mom's third-great-grand-parents. Once again, the Irish family naming pattern would come to the rescue.

STEP FOUR

I researched Mary's ancestor Thomas, filling in some missing infor-mation from her tree, and traced his family forward. In the 1901 census, he lived in Ireland next door to a John Butler. Both men shared the same family naming patterns. I located their birth certifi-cates and confirmed their parents were indeed John and Hannah, which I'd previously surmised from Thomas's children's names.

CONCLUSION

Based on our family trees and the percentage of DNA my mother and Mary share, I am quite confident that her Thomas's father, John, was a brother of my Michael Butler. Coincidentally both men married Byrne women, which will assist with further research. This DNA connection brings me one step closer to finding my mom's fourth-great-grandparents. Also, Mary informed me that we are related to the poet William Butler Yeats. As a writer, I find this pretty cool. It will lessen the blow should I learn we are not related to the actor Gerard Butler. I will continue searching for my Thomas, hoping to get a DNA hit from one of his descendants in the near future.

1 6

YOUR ANCESTORS WERE
DIVORCED? LUCKY YOU!

In the 1900 census, my ancestor James Flannery's marital status was noted as divorced. When I located his "wife" living with their son, her status was *widowed*. Interesting. I never did find their divorce record. Maybe they were never *legally* divorced, just emotionally divorced. But this discovery put divorce records on my genealogy radar. At that time if a person in the US wanted to obtain a divorce—especially a woman—she had to prove her spouse was guilty of adultery, abusive behavior, or abandonment. This usually required the testimony of witnesses in court, which could be a gold mine of information.

You will generally find divorce records on file at county courthouses or state archives. I've never located ones I needed online. However, you might find an index, depending on the state. Despite popular belief that divorces were uncommon back in those days, I've researched numerous divorced couples. If you feel an ancestor might have been divorced, it's definitely worth checking out.

The following are several helpful details I've found in court transcripts for three couples divorced in Chicago from 1892 to 1924.

RELATIVES' NAMES AND ADDRESSES

The witnesses turned out to be relatives, and their names and addresses assisted me with further genealogical research. In two cases the women filing for divorce lived with one of the witnesses.

INFORMATION ABOUT CHILDREN

The record will note if children were living with a parent or relative —possibly one you didn't know about. It will state the number of children and how many were alive. If the couple had deceased children you were unaware of, and names aren't mentioned, you'll want to locate their birth or death records.

A WOMAN'S MAIDEN NAME

The court asked the women if they wanted to take back their maiden names. They all replied yes and provided these surnames. This helped me confirm that Bertha Watson's maiden name was indeed Youngren, not Conners, as her son James stated on his marriage record. This assisted me in locating Bertha after she divorced and remarried.

PLACES OF EMPLOYMENT

Discovering my Watson ancestor was a steamfitter was critical in tracing my family in Chicago.

FUTURE SPOUSE'S NAME

If one spouse accused the other of adultery, they were required to provide the lover's name. I was able to locate a woman in future records because she married the man with whom she'd allegedly had the affair.

MARRIAGE DATE AND LOCATION

This is very helpful if you've been unable to locate a marriage certificate. Also, knowing the marriage date is important because couples usually began having children soon after they married—so you can estimate when the first child was born.

A SPOUSE'S LAST KNOWN ADDRESS

In one instance, the man had moved from Chicago back to his hometown in Ohio. He had a common surname. I'd never have found him if I hadn't known he'd relocated.

17

SHIP PASSENGER LISTS:

HELPING YOU EMBARK ON GENEALOGICAL RESEARCH

Finding your ancestor's name on a ship manifest can be hit or miss in the US prior to the opening of Ellis Island in 1892, when arrival records became more legible and detailed. I've been unable to locate my ancestor Patrick Coffey on a manifest despite knowing his arrival month and year into the Port of New York. Hundreds of Patrick/Pat/P. Coffeys, farmers from Ireland, emigrated during that same time period. Locating the ship manifests for my Irish ancestors Patrick Daly, Eliza Butler, and John McDonald was worth the time-consuming search.

Patrick Daly noted that his destination was Monroe, Wisconsin. Besides debunking family folklore that he'd been a stowaway on a potato boat, this confirmed he likely knew someone in Monroe. After a bit of research, I discovered that his maternal Collentine uncles lived in that area. My mother never knew she was related to the Collentines in her hometown fifteen miles away. For decades her family collected their daily mail from the postmistress, Margaret Collentine, without having known her relation.

My ancestor Eliza Butler emigrated from County Wicklow at the age of sixteen with her father and two siblings. Her mother had apparently died in Ireland or during the voyage. Eliza disembarked the ship with her future husband, John McDonald, and his family. This confirmed that their marriage record would be located in the States, not in Ireland. Also, according to family folklore, John and Eliza had met during their long voyage to America.

John emigrated with a Thomas, Walter, Ellen, and Patrick McDonald. Wanting to learn their relationships to John, I searched for two-year-old Patrick's baptismal record in Ireland based on his mother having been Ellen and his father either Thomas or Walter. I found a Patrick born in County Wicklow to a Thomas McDonald and Ellen Bracken. A death record later confirmed this was the maiden name of the Ellen traveling with my John. The couples' child Patrick had died before the 1860 US Census, during which time a newborn son, Patrick, had joined the family. Patrick was obviously an important family name. It confirmed that Thomas's father's name was undoubtedly Patrick, the same as my John's father, so they were likely brothers.

In the 1860 census, Thomas and Ellen's family lived next to Eliza and John McDonald. However, Walter was nowhere to be found. Despite the ship manifest having recorded his age and occupation as a shoemaker, I still haven't located him. Yet he was an important clue. Thomas named his fourth-born son Walter, meaning Walter from the ship was likely a brother. Knowing these relatives enabled me to obtain their vital records and obituaries, which assisted with the family tree.

In addition to the manifest noting Walter was a shoemaker, it had that Eliza was a dressmaker, John a weaver, and Ellen a cotton spin-ner. These were different trades than the farming livelihood they had in the States. I knew the Butlers were from Avoca Valley, County Wicklow, a large mining area. Their occupations in Ireland led me to believe that they'd worked at Avoca Mills, established in 1723 so farmers could spin and weave their wool to clothe local miners. (This also had me questioning family folklore that Eliza and John had never met before setting sail to America.) The Butler men recorded as laborers on the manifest were quite likely miners. Today Avoca provides brightly colored woolen goods to its quaint shops throughout Ireland, including the original one in the town of Avoca. I have numerous scarves, blankets, and socks with the label **AVOCA, The Mill, Est. in Ireland 1723**. What an interesting tidbit to include in the family's biography! (You can check out the lovely Avoca store at www.avoca.com.)

My ancestors sailed to America from
Cobh, County Cork, Ireland

18

MAPPING OUT YOUR ANCESTORS

When I went to a historical society to research naturalization papers, I sat at a table with a large map displayed under a glass top. I learned this was an 1860s Wisconsin plat map that detailed land ownership boundaries. The owner's name was written on the land parcel, giving you a visual of your ancestor's homestead and the surrounding neighbors. This was a great discovery. Since then I've often used plat maps in my research.

The maps have helped me to determine my ancestors' neighbors, which I then researched. I found my ancestor John McDonald living next door to a Matthew McDonald, who was likely a relative and a new lead. Also, if you've been unable to locate an ancestor in the census, possibly due to a document or transcription error, find his neighbors on the plat map. Look up the neighbors in the census, and you might find your relative living next to them or at least in close proximity.

A plat map can help you narrow down someone's death date, which is especially helpful from 1880 to 1900, since the 1890 US Census was destroyed in a fire. On an 1890 land map, I found my Patrick Coffey's widow's name noted, so Patrick had died prior to that time. Also, the home's location within a township can help determine what church the family likely attended, and thus their burial location. My Coffeys' land was on the edge of the township, so I looked at a map for the bordering township and found they'd owned twice as much land as I'd thought.

You can find plat maps for 1860 to 1918 on Ancestry.com. Over five million federal land title records issued from 1788 to the present, along with plat maps, are included at www.glorecords.blm.gov/default.aspx. I learned that my relative Thomas Butler had purchased land in 1855, so I can now check the county courthouse for land records, which might help me trace him.

Another important map I've utilized is from Ireland's Griffith's Valuation, www.askaboutireland.ie/griffith-valuation. This was the first full-scale valuation of property in Ireland taken from 1847 to 1864. The purpose was to establish the value of all privately held lands and buildings in both rural and urban areas in order to determine a rental rate for each unit of property. The original document lists the landlords' and tenants' names. At that time, rather than owning the land they lived on and farmed, Irish tenants leased property from English landlords. The other tenants would have been your ancestors' neighbors.

I used the map to locate my Coffeys' ancestral home in County Westmeath. Family members and I visited the current owners, who invited us in for a three-course meal and lively conversation. They were quite appreciative to learn their home's history. My James Coffey had passed his *leased* land and buildings to his son John in 1874. John continued to lease the property until 1884, when he immigrated to Chicago. At that time the lease passed from the Coffeys to an unrelated family, which held it for a short period. It was then leased by the Doyle family—the current owners—who was the first family given the opportunity to purchase the land in the early 1900s following a series of Land Acts. Interesting that the house has been occupied almost solely by the Coffey and Doyle families for over two hundred years.

Chicago is a great example of the need for maps in genealogical research. I've used city ward maps, community area name maps, and other maps to assist with the street renumbering that took place in 1909. This FamilySearch page has a great overview of useful genealogical maps in the United States, www.familysearch.org/wiki/en/United_States_Maps. The site also has maps for other countries, such as Canada, Germany, England, and more.

The Sanborn Map Co. created maps to evaluate potential fire hazards in communities, even small villages where many of my ancestors lived. These maps provided insurance agents with the size, placement, square footage, and building materials of properties. First drawn in 1867, the maps are quite detailed, using symbols and color coding and noting the names and locations of businesses, churches, and government buildings. Viewing a map of my ancestors' village enabled me to envision the corner market where they'd shopped. The factory or businesses where they might have worked. And the opera house that had entertained them with numerous performances. The maps help bring your ancestors' communities to life. The Library of Congress offers a large digitized collection of the Sanborn maps, www.loc.gov/collections/sanborn-maps.

19

HOW ONE CLUE HELPED ME
SOLVE A TEN-YEAR
FAMILY MYSTERY

I've mentioned previously that I've been searching for ten years for my ancestor Eliza Butler's three brothers—John, Thomas, and Michael—who emigrated in 1852 from Ireland to southwestern Wisconsin. I've since had a *major* breakthrough thanks to perseverance and one random clue.

While perusing Ancestry.com forums, I came across Lucy, who was researching the same Butler family as I was. Her post was several years old, but I reached out to her and shared my family tree. She later contacted me with several questions, which I happily answered. I asked her if by chance she'd ever located my Eliza's three brothers. She responded that she'd possibly located one. However, she had been unable to confirm the connection.

She'd found a John Butler who had lived in Marquette County, located in Michigan's Upper Peninsula, which borders on northern Wisconsin. He and his roommates were miners, same as my Butlers. Several of the men were Cavanaughs—my John's sister Mary had married a Cavanaugh. One roommate's descendant is a DNA match of Lucy's. Another was the son of a Winnie *Butler* Mulligan. This was the first I'd heard of Winnie Butler, but I assumed the older woman was likely John's aunt. My mind reeled. I was confident this was my long-lost rellie John Butler, living with relations and friends from his family's homeland.

Unfortunately, I was unable to locate John after the 1870 census. However, I searched the census for his brothers and found a Thomas living nearby, a miner, born the same year as mine in Ireland. His children's names matched my Butlers' family naming pattern. Lucy had come across the man but wasn't familiar with the Irish family naming pattern, so she hadn't made the connection.

Within a few hours I'd pieced together Thomas's family, including nine children and their descendants. The death certificate for Thomas's firstborn son noted his birthplace as the Wisconsin town where my Butlers had lived. I found Thomas and several of his sons listed in Michigan's 1890s Marquette County Directory, living in Ishpeming. His son Edward worked for an opera house. Out of curiosity—which is a necessary trait for a genealogist—I looked at the county's business directory. I discovered a nearby McDonald's Opera House. I gasped with excitement.

My ancestor Eliza Butler had married a McDonald, as had her sister. Only a few Butlers and McDonalds lived in this small community. It couldn't be a coincidence, could it? The city directory listed Donald McDonald as the proprietor of the opera house. My mom is a DNA match with descendants of a Donald McDonald born in Scotland.

Next on my to-do list is to research Donald McDonald's family and Winnie Butler Mulligan—the mother of one of John Butler's roommates. This one clue not only helped me solve a ten-year mystery, but it has inspired several new leads. Moral of this story: no matter how minor a clue seems, it may lead to a major breakthrough in research.

20

A TEA TOWEL CAN HELP
DETERMINE YOUR
ANCESTORS' ORIGINS

Several years after I embarked on my ancestry research, I came across a nifty tea towel in a souvenir shop—an Ireland map indicating the origin locations of a hundred Irish surnames. I've since seen similar towels for Scottish clan names and English surnames. The Irish towel was spot on. My Cullens came from County Wexford. My Dalys from Westmeath. My Butlers from southern Wicklow, near the Kildare border. According to the map, the McDonald name originated in Donegal, whereas my family history had them from Wicklow.

When my McDonald family emigrated from Ireland to America, the ship manifest noted the family as Scottish. However, the US Census later documented their place of birth as Ireland. Had my ancestor been born in Ireland but identified with his Scottish ancestry? Donegal was colonized largely by the Scottish in the 1600s as part of England's Ulster Plantation system. When James I became king of England, Ireland, and Scotland, the northern part of Ireland was the most Catholic and least anglicized area of the island. He decided this needed to be rectified and had loyal English and Scottish Protestants settle the area. Many believe the plantations were a long-term cause of the partition between Roman Catholics and those who belonged to the Church of Ireland. (The Church of Ireland [Anglican] was the official state church under English rule from 1690 to 1870 and is still the dominant church in Northern Ireland. The majority of the Northern Irish have forefathers who emigrated from England and Scotland, whereas the Republic of Ireland is traditionally Roman Catholic.) Had my McDonalds originally immigrated to Donegal as part of the colonization, then eventually migrated down to Wicklow? Something I'll consider for future research.

Too bad I hadn't seen this towel when I began my research and had little knowledge of my ancestors. However, the map may help me pinpoint the homeland of my Watson family ancestors, including the Turneys, Connollys, and McCarthys. If you have no idea what area of Ireland (or Scotland, England, or other country) your ancestors came from, start with a tea towel. Also, here are several websites featuring Ireland surname maps, many of which are based on the mid-1800s, and Scottish clan maps. I'm sure there are similar maps for other countries. Add these to my previous list of useful maps for genealogical research.

Irish surnames:

www.irishcentral.com/roots/irish-surname-maps

www.swilson.info/sdist.php

www.barrygriffin.com/surname-maps

Interesting tidbits on the top 100 Irish surnames:

www.irelandbeforeyoudie.com/ranked-top-100-irish-surnames-and-meanings

Scottish clans:

www.highlandtitles.com/scottish-clans-and-families/#map

21

GIVE IT THE OLD COLLEGE TRY:

HOW A SCHOOL YEARBOOK HELPED ME
SOLVE A THIRTY-YEAR FAMILY MYSTERY

I often discuss the need to be creative when conducting genealogical research and attempting to solve family mysteries. In 1988 after my grandpa Watson died, my dad was sorting through Grandpa's belongings and came across a divorce certificate. My dad hadn't known about his father's previous marriage. When he questioned his mother, she merely shrugged it off. Having been an only child, my dad was curious if he possibly had a half sibling somewhere. This was long before the advent of ancestry DNA tests. My dad hadn't kept the certificate but recalled that the divorce had taken place in Minnesota. A few years later, he went there to search for papers detailing the divorce terms, such as child custody and support. He came up empty.

Last year my sister and I were sitting at the kitchen table discussing family secrets uncovered when someone dies, including our grandpa's divorce. I opened my laptop and searched Ancestry.com for my grandpa's first marriage record. He had a unique name, so when an Indiana marriage record popped up with his name and birth date, I checked it out. We weren't aware of any connections he'd had to Indiana, yet possibly his ex-wife had. At the time of the marriage, he'd been attending college in Iowa, so I thought he might have met his first wife there. I'd previously attached the links for his college yearbooks to his ancestry page, so I searched through them for the woman's name on the marriage certificate. She'd indeed attended the same college, confirming this was my grandpa's marriage record.

I found the woman's family tree online. She'd remarried fifteen years after divorcing my grandpa and had three children. No previous marriage, or children from one, were noted. It was likely that her family, same as mine, hadn't known about the marriage. If the marriage had ended poorly for the young couple, had they possibly put a child up for adoption? Unless a half sibling shows up as a DNA match for my dad, we'll never know.

Even though we were disappointed not to discover that my dad has a half sibling, the yearbook contained some interesting information. I found pictures of my grandpa with the football team and his fraternity. Three-time Pulitzer Prize–winner Carl Sandburg had been a guest speaker at the college. Not only did the yearbooks help me solve a thirty-year family mystery, but they gave me a much better picture of my grandpa in his younger years.

22

COUNTY DIRECTORIES:

FINDING RURAL ANCESTORS

I previously touched on using the Marquette County Directory (Michigan) while researching my Butler and McDonald ancestors. I'm now going to discuss it in further detail and the wealth of information it contains. A helpful aspect of a county directory is that it lists people living in small communities, not just big cities.

If you're unable to locate an ancestor's death record or obituary, check a directory's residential listing. It often included deaths, such as this one: Ronald McDonald, aged 84 years, died May 15, 1900. A wife was rarely listed unless she was the head of a household, in which case it might note the following: Winnie Butler (widow of Michael), occupation, address. I found that Charles McDonald was *removed* to Calumet, Michigan. I'm not sure if that referred to him having relocated or having been buried there, as a burial was often referred to as a removal. Either way, it can help track someone who suddenly disappeared from an area.

Look beyond the residential listings. A directory's front pages might include city, town, county, and federal government employees, as well as employees of the fire and police departments and public schools. You may find an ancestor was an officer or member of a club, organization, or society—including secret societies such as the Freemasons. Church and cemetery listings can help you locate older and abandoned cemeteries. And knowing the local newspapers circulating at the time will help you locate family obituaries and news. Reminder: a paper's gossip column has helped me break through several brick walls.

Scan the business directory for your ancestor's name. Maybe he owned a business you weren't aware of, and if he had a partner, that person might have been a relative, especially in the case of bars, grocery stores, and restaurants. The business directory is a great place to locate women with professions such as dressmakers, milliners, and piano teachers. They often worked out of their homes, so their work address can link wives with husbands in the residential directory.

A county directory not only provides insight into many areas of an ancestor's life, but it can provide clues that lead you down a path to other historical documents.

23

CONNECTING THE FAMILY DOTS:

HOW LINKING CLUES
CAN LEAD TO ANSWERS

Raised by his stepfather, my grandpa Watson only knew his biological father's name and that he was a steamfitter in Chicago. After I located his father's historical records in Chicago, I traced the family back two generations to Montreal, Canada. I located James Watson and Bridget Connolly's Montreal marriage record from 1841 and their three children's baptismal records. (FYI, the Illinois death certificates for children James, Anna, and Margaret each noted a different mother's name. None of them were correct, which is likely because Bridget had died in Canada at a young age. This is a reminder that you should always have more than one source for ancestry information.)

James and Bridget's Presbyterian marriage record noted James was a soldier in Her Majesty's 23rd Regiment Fusiliers. I hired a genealogist to retrieve James's military documents from England's archives and learned he was born in 1811, in Pollokshaws, Scotland. Canada's 1851 census record noted Bridget was born in 1817 in Ireland. Excited to discover I had Irish ethnicity on my paternal side of the family, I began researching Bridget Connolly.

Bridget would likely have immigrated to Canada with family members prior to her marriage in 1841, so I reviewed Montreal's city directories. In 1820 only one Connolly was listed. By 1842 there were William, Patrick, and John *Conley* and Robert, Michael, and John *Connolly*. I mapped out their addresses, and based on the proximity of their residences and the variation in surname spellings, I concluded these six men were from two families.

Since Bridget was married in 1841, I focused on pre-1845 Connolly marriages. Unlike James and Bridget's Presbyterian marriage record containing little personal information, Catholic records for nineteen Connollys provided the couples' parents' names along with country and county of residence. If James and Bridget had been married Catholic, my research would have been done. There were thirteen sets of parents living in nine counties in Ireland. William, Patrick, and John Conley (later Connolly in the city directories, demonstrating the use of surname variations) were born to John Connolly and Honora Collier in County Tipperary, Ireland. Robert, Michael, and John Connolly were not married Catholic, so their church records didn't include any family information. I'd narrowed it down to two Connolly families but couldn't be sure which one Bridget belonged to.

If Bridget was the daughter of Honora Collier, why had she named her firstborn daughter Anna? I also couldn't find a baptismal record for Bridget in Ireland, but I found ones for the three Connolly boys born to John and Honora. Yet my gut told me this was Bridget's family, so I added this Connolly family to my tree on Ancestry.com with a note that verification was needed.

Down the road, my dad had a DNA match with a descendant of a Collier family from Templetouhy, County Tipperary, Ireland—where John and Honora Connolly had lived. Their connection was linked via DNA ThruLines, which matched my dad's family tree to the Collier descendant's tree. While communicating with the newfound relation, she noted the name as Hanora rather than

Honora, and it suddenly dawned on me where Anna had come from. It was a nickname for Hanora, less frequently for Honora. Thankfully, I'd gone with my instinct that Bridget was the daughter of Honora Collier Connolly. (In Tip 28, I discuss how nicknames can cause confusion and brick walls.)

How Many Ancestors Do You Have?

Parents	2
Grandparents	4
Great-Grandparents	8
2nd Great-Grandparents	16
3rd Great-Grandparents	32
4th Great-Grandparents	64
5th Great-Grandparents	128
6th Great-Grandparents	256
7th Great-Grandparents	512
8th Great-Grandparents	1,024
9th Great-Grandparents	2,048
10th Great-Grandparents	4,096
11th Great-Grandparents	8,192
12th Great-Grandparents	16,384
13th Great-Grandparents	32,768
14th Great-Grandparents	65,536
15th Great-Grandparents	131,072

How many ancestors do you have?

24

HE'S NO JOE BLOW:

THE IMPORTANCE OF
SPONSORS AND WITNESSES

I am surprised by how often people overlook sponsors and witnesses in marriage and baptismal records when conducting genealogical research. Yet I doubt I paid them much attention in the beginning. These names have helped me piece together numerous ancestry lines since the people were typically family members. The following are some highlights of the important clues these people have provided me.

When my ancestors Honora Collier and John Connolly married in County Tipperary, Ireland, three Collier men, who I assumed were her brothers, witnessed the marriage. (Witnesses may also be first cousins, but more often I've found them to be siblings.) Were they there in full force to show their support or disapproval of the marriage? Hmm . . . This *one* record provided three siblings' names. These would be helpful in determining Honora's father's name, since the third-born son would have been named after his father. Right there I had three possibilities. However, I found it odd that there was no witness there on behalf of the groom, until I discovered a bonus marriage record.

I found a marriage record for this couple in John Connolly's townland within the same parish. The marriage in Honora's church didn't have a date in 1805, but it was in the middle of the listings, so I assumed it occurred around the same time as the July marriage noted in her husband's church. I've never come across two marriage records. At first glance I thought one might have been their marriage banns, once a common practice in the Catholic Church and the Church of Ireland. The banns—an announcement of the intent to marry—were read in a couple's church three Sundays in a row. The congregation then spread the news about the upcoming marriage throughout the community and local busybodies. It allowed parishioners the opportunity to voice any objection to the marriage, such as a preexisting marriage, lack of consent, or the couple being related within the prohibited degrees of kinship. However, upon further inspection, I determined the second record wasn't a banns announcement. The banns wouldn't have had witnesses.

Since a couple usually married in the woman's church, the record in John's church was likely a blessing by his priest. The list of witnesses on the second marriage document included one of Honora's brothers, one of John's brothers, and a John Brennan—an unfamiliar surname that must have been an important connection to the Connolly family. All this information from merely one marriage with two wedding records. The next time I find a marriage record, I'm going to be greedy and keep looking. There just might be a second one out there.

For this same Collier family, I perused twenty-five years of records online, reviewing the sponsors and witnesses. I came across three Edmond Colliers in my ancestor's parish. I needed to determine which one was Honora's brother. One of the Edmonds married a Mary Kennedy. Five years later, a Mary Kennedy was the witness for Honora's son's baptism. A Judith Collier and Thomas Kennedy (Kennedys were apparently an important family connection) were sponsors for another Collier child, and I later determined they were married. In Ireland a priest typically documented a woman's maiden name rather than her married one. However, I have found that is not *always* the case. It could depend on the parish. Also, a brother-in-law could be a sponsor, which has helped me determine a sister's married name.

I've been trying to confirm my dad's third-great-grandmother Mary Ann McCarthy's birth location in Ireland. A new lead appeared in the 1870s when I linked the siblings Hannah and Thomas McCarthy with my Watsons in Chicago. When Hannah McCarthy White baptized her son in Chicago, one of the sponsors was a Mary Cronin. In the 1800s the largest concentration of McCarthys was found in southwest Ireland, so that was where I began searching for Hannah's baptismal record. I came across a record in Killarney, County Kerry, for her approximate birth year, the mother Mary Cronin. If not the same Mary Cronin as the one in the Chicago baptismal record, quite likely a relation. However, coincidences occur more frequently than you would think in genealogical research, so I marked this as a *possible* baptismal certificate. I later confirmed it when I discovered Hannah's husband was also born in Killarney.

Witnesses' and sponsors' names can also help determine if family members were still living in the area or if they'd possibly emigrated, married, or died. Determining when a paper trail ends in one country can help you identify when it starts in another. I have had people go missing for years and then suddenly pop up as a sponsor. Checking baptismal and marriage records in the country the family immigrated to can help you confirm which family members relocated. If the sponsor or witness isn't related, he likely emigrated from the same area.

Church records are available online for many countries I've researched, including Ireland, England, Scotland, and Canada. Unfortunately, as I mentioned in a previous tip, it's rare to find church records online for the US. Priests often consider parish records confidential, even if the person has been deceased for a hundred years. I have obtained records by making a donation in person or via snail mail and also by reaching out to a local historian or parishioner who had an in. I kept trying and finally succeeded with one church when it changed priests. Genealogy is all about perseverance.

I'm currently checking every witness or sponsor noted in my family trees against my parents' DNA matches' trees with the same surnames. I've just begun the search, and I've already made several connections. Hopefully, these new discoveries lead to many more!

25

WILLS & PROBATE:

INSIGHT INTO FAMILIES, FINANCES, AND FEUDS

My first attempt at obtaining an ancestor's will was disheartening. I visited a courthouse in southwestern Wisconsin inquiring about a will for my relative who died in 1935, which is fairly recent in genealogical terms. It turned out that my ancestor had dementia at the time of his death, so his records had been destroyed. Seriously? His will was possibly drawn up years prior when he was still of sound mind. I was so upset that I told the clerk that the destruction of these records was wrong on many levels.

England's and Ireland's will indexes contain a lot of information in only a few sentences. This will get you started with the research while you are waiting to receive a copy of the actual document. A listing has the deceased's death date and address. It states a woman's marital status at the time of death: a spinster, widow, or married, including the husband's name. For a man, it gives his widow's name. If the executor isn't the spouse, it notes the person's name and occupation. If that person is a woman, it will give her husband's name. And last but not least, it discloses the estate's value.

Despite the wealth of information in an index, I've still ordered copies of wills to obtain even more details. One original document listed the deceased widow's two living children. Confirming the other three children had died, I then located their death records.

I once came across a will that listed more than twenty heirs to an estate. Most shared the deceased's surname, so if not his children, other family members. Several with different surnames turned out to also be related. I'd hit the genealogy jackpot.

When I was researching a potential Watson connection in Wisconsin, his paper trail ended with the 1860s US Census. Had he died? Death certificates were extremely rare at that time. Find a Grave is a great resource, but it's hit or miss if a volunteer has contributed the grave information you need. Eventually I located George Watson's will and probate record on Ancestry.com, which noted his death date. At the time of his death, he was living in Canada, but his Wisconsin estate was managed by a lawyer in the US. Had he moved to Ontario to be near my ancestor James Watson in Kingston?

The document noted that George was widowed. His married daughter, the executrix, was living in Canada along with four siblings. George's son appealed the will. His father's estate was valued at $12,500, almost $400,000 in today's dollar, and he'd received a meager $25, about $775 today. I guess the son took it harder than the three other siblings, who'd received the same amount. Whereas the executrix inherited the bulk of the estate, including eighty-six acres of land, livestock, and farm equipment. This spoke volumes about the family's dynamics.

The paperwork also included correspondence between George and his Wisconsin property's caretaker several years prior to his death. It detailed the amount the estate paid the caretaker to ensure nothing was stolen and to guard the apple trees from the scoundrel neighbor. I'm guessing there had been an ongoing dispute over the two men's plot lines. George also inquired if the Irish men had yet come for the potatoes. That made me smile. You never know what you might find in a will.

26

THE SOCIAL SECURITY DEATH INDEX TELLS ABOUT A PERSON'S LIFE

The US Social Security Death Index, 1935–2014, is a great way to verify if someone has died. The index is available on several sites, including Ancestry.com and FamilySearch. Currently, the Family-Search database only covers 1962–2014. The record will include the person's death date and his most recent address or at least the city or town. If a person doesn't come up in the index, try searching by his birth date. He might be listed under a different name, or there could have been an error in transcription. Having a person's death date and location makes it easier to find an obituary. However, a person's Social Security death record provides more information about his *life* than his *death*. The following are some examples.

TRACKS MOVEMENT

I discovered the index when I was helping a friend in Ireland search for descendants of his family, who'd immigrated to Galena, Illinois, in the 1800s. At that time the index merely provided the person's name and death location. I had to order the record, which is now available online. The woman I was attempting to locate was from Illinois, but the record was for a person who'd died in California. I crossed my fingers, hoping I was ordering the correct one. Thankfully, the original record noted that the card had been issued before 1951 in Illinois and provided the woman's birth date, confirming I'd found my missing person. Using her last-known California residence, I Googled the address and discovered her daughter living there. I put my Irish friend in touch with her. They are still corresponding.

BIRTH DATE AND LOCATION

In the census, I've often found a family's children all listed with the same birth location. Yet when I'm unable to locate one of the children's birth records, I question the accuracy of the information. Following additional research, I've frequently concluded that a child was born in a different state or country. These errors might have occurred due to the enumerator's or informant's haste or laziness. However, if the person himself supplied the incorrect information, maybe he'd assumed he was born in the same location as his siblings and was never told differently. The correct information was generally given on a Social Security application since people were more concerned about the accuracy of a legal financial document.

PARENTS' NAMES

This is a great resource for verifying a person's parents' names. The mother's maiden name is often noted, and it's likely correct since it was provided by the parents or the person themselves. When a distraught family member supplies information for a loved one's death certificate, he often isn't thinking clearly and gives incorrect information. The person also might not have known his mother's maiden name—like the three Watson siblings mentioned in a previous tip whose death certificates all noted a different mother's name, not one of which was correct.

WOMEN'S SURNAME CHANGES

The "Notes" section will document a woman's surname changes. This is helpful for tracking female ancestors. In the 1940 census, my ancestor James Watson had a stepdaughter Harriet. Her Social Security death record noted her new married surname in 1948. If she had later divorced and taken back her maiden name, or remarried, the name would have been listed.

NAME VARIATIONS

Besides documenting women's surname changes, a record will list various spellings for a person's name and known aliases.

27

TEN WAYS TO DETERMINE DEATH DATES

I've touched on a few of these resources in previous tips. However, I believe it's beneficial to have them all listed in one spot under the topic of determining death dates.

1. DEATH CERTIFICATES

This is the most obvious one, yet one of the most difficult documents to obtain. Locating US death records prior to 1900 can be hit or miss and varies widely depending on the state. Wisconsin law required counties to register birth, marriage, and death events with state officials starting in 1852, but the law was not strictly enforced until roughly 1880. Yet I've had a difficult time locating certificates prior to 1900. And the amount of information included varies drastically. Sometimes more information is included on certificates from rural Wisconsin than Chicago. Too busy recording deaths in the city to document details?

2. OBITUARIES

This might sound crazy because if you don't have the death date, wouldn't you spend days searching years of newspapers to locate an obituary? However, local libraries and genealogical or historical societies often have an online database of their obituaries. I was recently in need of a death date and went online to see if the library in that area might have an obituary available—usually for a nominal fee, and the database included the death date. An obituary is also a great way to find a spouse's death date. For example, it'll often note that the person had been preceded in death ten years prior by the spouse, providing an estimated date on where to begin searching for a spouse's obituary.

3. GRAVESTONES

Find a Grave or BillionGraves are great resources. However, volunteers contribute the information, so not every cemetery or every grave within a cemetery are included. If the site has your ancestor's grave, not only will you find the death date but possibly family members linked to the page. I have also found obituaries and family bios on a person's memorial page. If a link to surrounding graves is provided, you can check out the neighbors and see if any names look familiar. If the site doesn't include your needed grave, contact a local genealogical society. If they don't have cemetery transcriptions, a volunteer might be able to assist. You can also find a volunteer at Random Acts of Genealogical Kindness.

4. SOCIAL SECURITY INDEX

The US Social Security Death Index, 1935–2014, is a great way to verify if someone has died. The record will include the person's death date, location, birth date, and other personal information. If you have no idea where or when a person died, you can search for Social Security death records by birth date.

5. LAND TAX RECORDS

These records might be housed at regional or state archives or county courthouses. Even if annual taxes were collected, that doesn't mean all the records have survived. An 1872 tax roll listed the number of acres Patrick Coffey owned as well as the location and valuation. In 1880 Mrs. Coffey was listed rather than Patrick, so he'd died sometime between 1872 and 1880. At least that narrowed it down.

6. PLAT MAPS

A plat map shows ownership boundaries delineated by tax parcel property lines. The owner's name is written on the land parcel. Patrick Coffey was noted on an 1860 map, but by the next available map in 1890, the land was in his wife Margaret's name.

7. GOSSIP COLUMNS

The gossip column is a gold mine of information, not merely a bunch of fluff contributed by the local busybodies. It often notes who was in town visiting for a funeral. It might take a while to locate a death this way, but you will have fun catching up on the area's gossip.

8. WILLS

Wills and probate records almost always include a death date. They are also a great way to learn what other family members were dead or alive at that time.

9. VOTER REGISTRATION

This is a great resource if your ancestor lived in a city. Many rural locations didn't have registration until recent years. Determining when a person stopped voting can help pinpoint his death date. This record also documents a person's birth location, term of residence in that county and state, and whether or not he was a naturalized citizen. If naturalized, it noted when and where the process took place, including if it was at a state, county, or city courthouse. Knowing the precise location can be helpful when searching for naturalization papers.

10. CITY DIRECTORIES

Same as voter registration records, when a person no longer appears in a city directory, they'd likely died or moved. A widow often listed her name after her husband's death until she remarried, such as: Mary (widow of John), address. She may have listed prior to his death if she operated a business out of the home, such as milliner or piano teacher. Maybe a woman had also used this as a sort of dating directory, wanting men to know that she was now available.

28

WAS SHE MARY, MOLLY, OR POLLY?

IDENTIFYING UNUSUAL NICKNAMES

My given name, Elizabeth, has over a hundred possible nicknames, including mine, Beth, and my pen name, Eliza. Those who prefer a new twist on an old name might use Liesel, Birdie, or Zella. How about Elspeth? I'd never heard the name until I started conducting genealogical research. It was, and maybe still is, a popular Scottish form of Elizabeth. Having a traditional name, I share a name with numerous ancestors, including an Elizabeth Darcy Coffey. Maybe that's why I'm such a huge fan of Elizabeth Bennett and Mr. Darcy in Jane Austen's *Pride and Prejudice*. I've talked about how the traditional Irish family naming pattern has helped me piece together family trees. On the flip side, obscure nicknames, all female in these cases, have caused me to hit several brick walls.

The Dalys were the first family line I researched. Patrick Daly's birth record noted his mother as Sarah Collentine. I later found Sarah's birth record, and her mother was Sally Flynn. My mom mentioned that Sarah was her grandma Sadie Daly's given name. Learning that Sally and Sadie were both nicknames for Sarah should have taught me early on to be aware of nicknames. However, these variations of Sarah at least made some sense to me. It was the ones that didn't that tripped me up.

When researching my Coffeys in Ireland, I documented all Coffey baptisms in the area I believed was my ancestors' homeland, hoping they might turn out to be related. You'll read in the Coffey Case Study that learning Polly is a nickname for Mary helped me solve my Coffey family mystery. Supposedly, Polly is derived from Molly, another unfamiliar nickname for Mary.

I've previously mentioned the three Watson siblings having different mothers noted on their death certificates, none of which had the correct name, Bridget Connolly. I recently researched the incorrect women's names, hoping one had a family tie. Wrong information on historical documents often held a thread of truth. One had the mother's first name as Delia. Deciphering her last name wasn't easy. It looked like Grieve, a Scottish name. I hadn't run across a Delia or a Grieve in my research. In the 1920s, at the time of this person's death, the name Delia had been popular in the US. Maybe the census informant had Americanized a traditional name. I checked names for which Delia was a nickname, and Bridget came up. How do you get Delia from Bridget? Since the actual mother's name was Bridget Connolly, I assume that was the thread of truth in the document. However, I'm keeping my eyes open for the last name Grieve. My dad has several DNA matches containing Grieves in their trees, so it might indeed have been a family name at some point.

It took me forever to locate Michael Butler and Eleanor Byrne's marriage record because she was documented as Nelly, he as Mick. These are more common nicknames than many of the previous ones, but they still didn't come up in a search. I finally discovered the record while reviewing the original church registers online. Their children's baptismal records noted her name as Eleanor. The couple had been married in a different parish, where they'd likely grown up and were known by their nicknames. This is a reminder that if you can't locate a record in a search, review the original registers and documents for the estimated time period.

Most genealogy search sites provide a "Sounds Like" or "Soundex" option. These are available when searching last names, but not first names. It often wouldn't help anyway since, for example, Delia doesn't sound a thing like Bridget. What do you do if you can't locate a person who used some obscure nickname? If searching for a marriage record, I'll use both persons' surnames and no first names or merely one of the first names. Or I'll transpose the names for one or both of the persons. I try similar tricks for other records.

Now when I search for a document, I check for every possible first-name variation. That becomes difficult when you are searching for a name like Elizabeth, which has loads of possible nicknames. Going by Elizabeth, Eliza, and Beth, I might one day be a genealogist's nightmare.

29

TRACING YOUR ANCESTORS VIA THEIR OCCUPATIONS

In a previous tip, I mentioned that a ship manifest listed my Butler and McDonald ancestors' occupations as laborer, weaver, shoemaker, and cotton spinner. Shortly after learning their professions, I was visiting their homeland, Avoca Valley, County Wicklow, Ireland, where I happened upon a plaque memorializing local miners. My ancestors had immigrated to southwestern Wisconsin, a big lead-mining area. I'd eventually located several of the Butler men in a mining area in Michigan's Upper Peninsula bordering northern Wisconsin. Upon further research of southern Wicklow, I determined that several family members had likely worked at Avoca Mills, established in 1723 so farmers could spin and weave their wool to clothe local miners, including Butler men.

Before departing their homeland, emigrants often had a final destination in mind, which was frequently linked to their occupations. I was later reviewing the manifest and noticed other passengers who'd worked in textile production, including another Butler and McDonald family. How had I missed that? More clues to research!

My ancestors James Watson and John Turney emigrated from Scotland and Ireland, respectively, as soldiers in Her Majesty's Military. A military profession is great for tracking people. Discharge and pension papers will usually detail a soldier's rank, military unit, and most importantly the periods and locations of service. Upon enrolling in the military, my ancestor James Watson went from Glasgow, Scotland, to County Down, Ireland, to Montreal, Canada, and finally to Kingston, Ontario, where he retired. Kingston is located on the eastern end of Lake Ontario, at the beginning of the St. Lawrence River leading out to the Atlantic. This made the city a military and trade hub. It was no surprise many of the residents' occupations revolved around the waterway.

John Turney's death record noted he was a retired sailor. That was news to me. In the 1871 Canada Census, his occupation was merely laborer, a bit vague. However, his daughter was a maid on a vessel. His three sons were steamfitters. James Watson Jr. was also a steamfitter. Possibly on a *steam*ship? I finally took the time to learn that steamfitters are pipe fitters who specialize in high-pressure liquid or gas piping that carry substances such as steam. They performed maintenance and installations on boiler, ventilation, and heating systems. That would have been a trade obtained and performed in mainly urban industrial areas rather than rural ones.

Steamfitters were a specialized niche even in Chicago. By 1870 the Turney men, along with their sister Eliza, who'd married James Watson Jr., had moved to the city and established a steam-fitting company. The following year, the Great Chicago Fire destroyed more than 17,000 wooden buildings. Watson and Turney relatives emigrated from Ireland and Scotland to work in the family business and help rebuild Chicago. Upon searching the 1872 city directories for our family surnames, I found many new arrivals working as steamfitters. Tracing relatives emigrating in the 1870s was a bit easier than tracing those who'd arrived in Canada forty years earlier. Chicago didn't have a steamfitter union at that time, but the Illinois Labor History Society might be a great resource for family information.

I had discovered a possible relation, Charles Watson, a steamfitter, in the 1892 Chicago city directory. The 1900 US Census listed several Charles Watsons living in Chicago, but none were steamfitters. However, one was a railroad conductor. Another Watson was a trackman for a steam railroad. If steamfitters worked on *steam*ships, they likely worked on *steam* railroads. When tracking ancestors via their professions, be sure to consider their transferable job skills.

My dad and his beagle, Ike, volunteer at a veterans' nursing home. One day while making the rounds, he met a James Watson. My father mentioned our family's long line of James Watsons and suggested the man's son, and family historian, reach out to me. For the past few years, Jon and I have been collaborating on Watson research, discovering several shared DNA matches. While reviewing a county plat map in Vermont, I noticed that his Irish ancestor lived near a flax mill. Interesting. There was a high probability that the person had emigrated from Ulster, where he'd been a linen weaver. (Ulster is now comprised of Northern Ireland and three counties from the Republic of Ireland: Cavan, Donegal, and Monaghan.)

In the eighteenth century, Ulster's linen industry grew to prominence. At its height almost a third of all flax spinning mills were located in Belfast, responsible for producing over half of Ireland's linen output and a third of the world's flax supplies. Spinning wheels were awarded based on the number of acres planted. People who planted one acre were awarded four spinning wheels, and those growing five acres were awarded a loom. In the Irish Linen Board's 1796 Flax Growers List, half the Watson families lived in County Tyrone. A great place for Jon to start looking for his ancestors.

Occupations not only give insight into what brought people to a certain location but also why they left an area. While I was helping a friend conduct research in County Hertfordshire, England, I discovered that her ancestors had been straw plaiters. In the eighteenth and nineteenth centuries, straw plaiting was a popular cottage industry. It employed thousands of people—mainly women and children—in the counties of Bedfordshire, Buckinghamshire, and Hertfordshire, all located near London. The men labored in straw fields or were hawkers, selling the finished products at local markets. Straw plaiting was a method of manufacturing textiles by braiding straw to produce items such as roof thatching, table mats, baskets, and bonnets. Due to cheaper imports from China, the straw-plaiting industry had pretty much died out by 1900. Rather than relocating to Asia and continuing their straw-plaiting careers, my friend's ancestors moved to London and reinvented themselves with new jobs as domestic servants.

How are you supposed to trace your ancestors via their occupations if they were all farmers or general laborers, both common professions in the 1800s and 1900s? Remember, John Turney was listed as a laborer when he'd actually been a sailor. And many farmers supplemented their income by other means. Once again why you need to obtain every possible historical record for your ancestors. You never know what you might discover from merely one of those documents.

30

DON'T FORGET ABOUT
THE LITTLE GUYS:

UTILIZING LOCAL LIBRARIES AND
GENEALOGICAL SOCIETIES FOR RESEARCH

Why begin your ancestry research with one of the giants like Ancestry.com or FamilySearch when a local library or genealogical society may have all the information you need in one spot? The following merely touches on the benefits of researching at the local level.

FAMILY RESEARCH DONATIONS

Many people contribute family history information to their local historical or genealogical organizations. I was recently perusing a website with a research index listing over six hundred family surnames. It noted the contributor's family relation or the volunteer who'd compiled the information. Family files included ancestry trees, copies of family photos, correspondence, probate records, stories, obits, and even a family diary—possibly juicier than the local newspaper's gossip column. Even if no family research has yet been donated, a volunteer might be able to put you in touch with a potential relation.

I have a distant cousin who has a half dozen family scrapbooks filled with newspaper clippings of obituaries, wedding announcements, and other events dating back a hundred years. While she was growing up, each weekend her mother would sit the children down at the kitchen table to paste clippings in the scrapbook. Having no children, my cousin will likely one day donate the books to a local organization.

ACCESS TO AN AREA EXPERT

A baptismal record for James Watson, born 1811 in Ireland, noted his father was a soldier in the Donegal Regiment. After a bit of quick research, I learned that the regiment was stationed in Letterkenny, County Donegal. I contacted the Letterkenny Historical Society, and the gentleman who responded provided a wealth of information on the regiment, including a research paper he'd written. He also informed me that a roster listing soldiers was on file at the National Library of Ireland. He has been an excellent resource.

RESEARCH ASSISTANCE

Librarians or volunteers can search their archives' noncirculating holdings that can't be found on research sites, such as local school records, family papers, scrapbooks, business records, yearbooks, and vintage photograph collections. If the information you need isn't on file, volunteers will often visit local cemeteries or the courthouse to obtain records or transcribe gravestones for a nominal donation.

When I conduct in-person research, the societies often have me complete a form detailing my family area of interest to be included in a binder, enabling researchers to collaborate.

CEMETERY TRANSCRIPTIONS

It's rare that a society doesn't have at least some of the local cemeteries transcribed. Remember, BillionGraves and Find a Grave are not inclusive of all burials in every cemetery worldwide. And what about the graves without headstones to photograph? Many headstones are too weathered to read or have crumbled to the ground. Or if your ancestor leased a plot at a large cemetery, they possibly never had a headstone, or it had been removed. Local historians often search church burial registers for missing and damaged headstones to include in a transcription list.

ONLINE STORE

Area experts often publish books, cemetery transcriptions, and other items. The authors may also be a great resource for answering questions not addressed in their publications. I once bought a book with over a hundred biographies for early settlers in the area, including several of my families.

OBITUARIES

I was recently in need of a death date and went online to see if a local library might have an obituary. Their database index included obituaries for the past hundred years, and one could be requested for a small fee.

MAPS

My ancestor James Watson was from Pollokshaws, Scotland. Sadly, much of the town has been rebuilt since he left the area in the mid-1800s. However, the local historical society provides an online map with older points of interest still in existence. When visiting the town, we were able to walk in our ancestors' footsteps.

NEWSLETTER INDEX

Many genealogical societies offer monthly or quarterly newsletters to members. Past newsletters are often available to nonmembers. I have found indexes listing hundreds of newsletter articles going back fifty-plus years. Authored by local residents, the articles may include family biographies, how historical events impacted the area, and much more.

MEMBERSHIP

I've joined numerous historical and genealogical societies in my ancestors' hometowns. Membership may provide you access to members-only records, discounts on online store publications, a society newsletter, and priority research requests. Being a member demonstrates your interest in the area's history and enables you to build relationships with the organization's volunteers and members.

31

WALKING AMONG THE DEAD:

WHAT A CEMETERY CAN TELL YOU ABOUT YOUR ANCESTORS' LIVES

I mentioned previously that each spring family members and I make our annual trip to southwestern Wisconsin to decorate our ancestors' graves. I've located many of the graves since 2007, when I began conducting genealogical research. I share stories with everyone about our ancestors who immigrated to America, along with stories about more recent relatives. For example, my grandma Flannery was born in the valley behind a cemetery located on what was once part of our family's land. This is why we're related to half the small rural cemetery. And likely why a relative responsible for keeping parishioners cozy warm was forgiven for accidentally burning down the church when stoking the woodstove. The family helped rebuild the church and donated a lovely stained-glass window.

For your first cemetery visit, I recommend bringing along copies of your family trees to share with everyone, aluminum foil for transcribing hard-to-read tombstones, a camera or phone for taking photos, and water and sunscreen, which I never remember.

SAY CHEESE

I likely have more photos of me in Irish cemeteries than all the tourist attractions there combined. Take a photo of the cemetery's entrance so you know where the following gravestone pics were taken. Even most rural cemeteries have a sign at the entrance. If there isn't one, then stand back far enough for a good view of the location. Also take photos of the general area in large cemeteries, including a landmark, such as a unique grave. Most importantly, take headstone shots so you can transcribe the information later.

NETWORK

In a cemetery? I have chatted with numerous locals in cemeteries. In Ireland a nice man once escorted us from a village cemetery to a remote one located miles away in the middle of a sheep field. Old farm machinery and equipment resembling torture devices filled the deserted homestead's property and had us questioning our decision to follow a stranger to the secluded area. To our relief, it was legitimate. I actually corresponded with the man, who turned out to be a Gavigan. My ancestor Patrick Coffey's sister had remained in the area and married a Gavigan. You never know where you might encounter a distant relative.

MEET YOUR ANCESTORS' NEIGHBORS

For several years I searched for my Eliza Butler's sister and finally located her laid to rest two tombstones away from Eliza. Her married name had thrown me off. Check online or visit the local courthouse to determine the maiden names of the women's graves surrounding your ancestors' graves.

CHECK FOR BIRTH LOCATIONS, NOT MERELY DATES

Many immigrants included their country of origin on their tombstones. Of course, only one of mine did, or that would have taken all the fun out of research. However, it was common for the Irish to even note their home county. My Flannery ancestors are buried in an old cemetery with mostly Irish immigrants. I snapped pictures of all the ones from County Mayo since people tended to move to where they knew someone from their homeland.

DISCOVER UNKNOWN CHILDREN

You might find children you were unaware of buried next to their parents. Knowing the year each child was born and his spot within the family tree is critical for ethnicities—such as Irish, English, and Scottish—that adhered to a traditional family naming pattern. Adding one name could alter everyone's relation, especially if you discover a firstborn son or daughter, who would have been named after a grandparent.

FIND EXTENDED FAMILY MEMBERS

Search the entire cemetery for your surname, not merely the surrounding area, especially if it's an uncommon name in a rural area. My mother didn't think she was related to other Flannerys in nearby towns. However, my genealogical research confirmed that all the families descended from one family that came to the area in 1850. They'd originally settled twenty miles from my mom's hometown, and families slowly dispersed over the years. Once you've documented all shared surnames, use the oldest person's information to check online for a family tree or vital records that might provide a clue to a possible family connection.

TRAVEL BACK IN TIME

Most of my ancestors lived in rural areas both here and in Ireland. However, I had to venture to Chicago to research the graves for my Watson and Turney ancestors. Most Chicago death notices provided funeral and burial information. They'd announce where and when the carriage procession or funeral train would depart from for the cemeteries located outside the city. What a depressing train ride that must have been, loaded with grieving passengers.

Rosehill Cemetery on the northside of Chicago still has the casket elevator that raised the coffin from the train to the cemetery's ground level. The stables also still exist that once housed the horses that delivered the caskets to the burial sites. I was able to clearly envision my grieving ancestors' experience.

LOCATION, LOCATION, LOCATION

Many of my Chicago Watson ancestors merely leased burial sites for a set number of years, so no tombstones were erected, or temporary ones were removed when their leases ran out. When a lease is up, some cemeteries allow it to be renewed, while others do not if space is limited. Remains are either removed from the grave and placed in an ossuary (a container or room in which remains are stored), or the new tenant is placed atop the existing one. I'd never heard of such a thing. I have no children. Who would renew my lease? I better make darn sure I purchase a permanent plot. I'm obsessed with cemeteries, and the thought of being kicked out of one is a bit unsettling.

The Rosehill Cemetery office provided me a map detailing the location of my Turney ancestors' graves. It was a poorer area of the cemetery, and over the years grave markers had become buried beneath the grass. How sad was that? Yet I guess it wasn't as sad as my poor ancestors being evicted from their resting spots. The map directed me to the graves' locations using landmarks and the approximate number of steps to take in which direction. When I arrived at my final destination, I used my fingers to dig up a layer of soil and grass to reveal a small memorial plaque with my ancestor's name and death date. I cleaned the slabs and left flowers on the graves. I recommend adding a shovel to your list of cemetery supplies. Or maybe a spade. Carrying a shovel through a cemetery might attract a bit of unwanted attention.

Exploring a sheep-filled cemetery in
County Westmeath, Ireland

GO STRAIGHT TO THE SOURCE:

QUESTIONS TO ASK YOUR RELATIVES

We gave our grandma Watson a question-a-day calendar for her to record memories, such as her favorite Christmas present and what she wore to school. She returned it a year later with only 10 percent of the questions answered. This is why it's best to ask these questions in person to ensure you receive answers. And questions often lead to unexpected conversations about things you wouldn't have known to ask about. Your relatives' answers will also make a great addition to a family biography.

PSST. DO YOU KNOW ANY FAMILY SECRETS?

This is the most important question. I know it depends on your family dynamics and relatives' willingness to reveal skeletons in your family's closet, but it's worth a shot. If you're the family genealogist, people will be looking to you for answers when an unknown DNA connection suddenly pops up. I've had this happen several times, and I'm expecting a few more.

When my mom's cousin was young, she often found herself under the kitchen table or on the other side of the door when family secrets were being discussed. She was aware of an older relative's out-of-wedlock pregnancy and the child she'd given up for adoption. Since I'm the family historian and manage our DNA accounts, I'll likely be the one who connects with this child should he search for his biological parents. At least I'll be prepared with answers.

WOULD YOU BE OPEN TO TAKING A DNA TEST?

I currently manage, or co-manage, seven DNA accounts for family and friends. I regret not having my great-uncle take one, especially since he was interested in genealogy. Even if you aren't into genealogy, one day you might be, and it'll be too late. Thanks to traditional ancestry research, several years ago I connected with a Coffey relative in Ireland. I gave him a DNA test last year for Christmas. It's helped us discover more relations.

WHICH ANCESTORS EMIGRATED AND FROM WHERE AND WHEN? DID THEY EMIGRATE WITH OTHERS?

Sadly, I lost three of my four grandparents when I was in my twenties and focused on college and my future rather than the past. However, I heard family folklore about my ancestor Patrick Daly coming to America as a stowaway on a potato boat. I debunked that story when I found the ship manifest listing his name and final destination. Even though he hadn't been a stowaway, there were likely potatoes on the boat. There's usually a thread of truth to every family story. Speaking of which, this reminds me of my great-uncle telling me stories about old man Butler and his three daughters. How one had supposedly married a McAloon. I later determined it had been old man Butler's *grand*daughter who'd married a man with this surname. It was still a helpful clue, even if it wasn't spot on.

DID FAMILY MEMBERS STAY IN TOUCH WITH ANYONE FROM THEIR HOMELAND?

In 1875 my ancestor Patrick Daly and his brother Michael emigrated from Ireland to southwestern Wisconsin. When Michael returned to Ireland to bring his parents back to America, his mother refused to leave. Michael remained there, and the brothers never saw each other again. However, Patrick's daughter Sadie—my great-grandmother—corresponded with a daughter of Michael's. Sadly, we don't know which *one* of Michael's four daughters. We know they stayed in touch, because in the 1950s Sadie asked her son stationed at a military base in Germany to attend a family wedding in Ireland on her behalf. He chose to spend his free weekend hanging out with his buddies in Germany instead, a decision he said he later regretted. I'd give anything to read those letters between the two first cousins who'd corresponded despite never having met.

WHERE DID YOU LIVE WHILE GROWING UP?

Two relatives gave my mom and me tours of the area where our ancestors had lived, pointing out their previous homes. We visited the farm in southern Wisconsin where our Flannery family settled after emigrating from County Mayo, Ireland, and the two rural houses next door to each other where my grandparents first met. During the tour, I frantically jotted down notes and stories that I later typed up for my family history binders.

Besides knowing the locations of your parents' or grandparents' homes, don't take it for granted you know their birth locations. My nephew's passport application was denied because he had the incorrect birthplace for his mother, my sister. She'd been born in southwestern Wisconsin, but our family moved three hours north when she was two years old.

I always thought my grandpa Watson had been born and raised in the small town where my dad grew up. It was only after he'd died that I discovered he'd been born in Milwaukee and raised in Iowa, where he'd graduated from college. Another surprise was that my grandpa had attended college. I'd give anything to be able to sit and listen to his university-day stories.

WERE YOU NAMED AFTER A RELATIVE?

I wasn't, but I've come across many ancestors with the traditional name Elizabeth. I like to think they've been helping me solve their genealogical mysteries.

HOW DID YOU MEET YOUR SPOUSE?

My grandma and grandpa Watson met on a double date on which they weren't dating each other. A week later my grandpa called and asked out my grandma. I'm reminded of the movie *When Harry Met Sally*.

WHAT ARE SOME SPECIAL CHILDHOOD MEMORIES?

When my mom was young, her grandfather was laid out in a casket in the sunroom at home. He was a second-generation Irish American, and they still held traditional Irish wakes. I'm sure she was a bit traumatized at the time. However, she has a photo of him at his wake. You just never know what you might come across in an old family album.

HOW WERE YOU IMPACTED BY HISTORICAL EVENTS?

My grandma Watson lived in Milwaukee during the depression. When I asked how it had affected her, she explained how lucky she was to have maintained jobs during that devastating period.

WHERE DID YOU WORK?

My Watson grandparents were already retired when I was born. Thankfully, I once chatted with my grandma about her job as a factory supervisor in Milwaukee and where she used to go dancing until her feet hurt too badly to walk. My grandpa had been a 1950s US Census taker. I'll be looking for his handwriting when the census becomes public in April 2022. (Update: I viewed the 1950 census for my grandpa's district. He had the most legible handwriting I've ever seen in a census, and he documented detailed information. Yay, Grandpa Watson! He never dreamed that seventy-two years later I'd be sharing my pride in a book.)

My grandma Flannery was a switchboard operator, which made it easy for her children to call and bug her at work. Whenever I see an old-time photo or movie with an operator sticking a phone plug into a jack, I think of my grandma.

33

ONCE UPON A TIME. . .

WRITING A CAPTIVATING
FAMILY BIOGRAPHY

When I share a family tree with relatives, they either look confused or overwhelmed. Many people don't know their ancestors' names beyond their grandparents and are suddenly bombarded with generations of unfamiliar people. Ten years ago I wrote several three-to-four-page family biographies for a reunion. Turning the family trees into story format made it much easier and more interesting for people to comprehend. The following are some tips for writing an engaging biography that will give people a sense of connection to ancestors they never knew.

START WITH A BANG

Like with my fiction novels, I want to hook the reader right from the first sentence. Here is an example of how I put the Flannery family's immigration into the context of a historical event, the Great Famine.

> County Mayo experienced the largest exodus of any county
> in Ireland due to the potato famine. In 1841, there were over
> 400,000 people in Mayo. By 1851, there were fewer than

250,000 due to emigration and deaths. Thankfully, many of our Flannery clan survived the famine and sailed to America beginning in 1852. They initially settled in Baltimore, Maryland, to work on the B&O Railroad. In 1855, James Flannery worked as a railroad laborer earning $1 per day. This would have been a considerable amount more than the eight pence a day the average worker was making in Ireland.

INTEGRATE HISTORICAL DOCUMENTS

Here is how I took a mundane tax roll and turned it into a relatable story about the effect it likely had on our ancestor.

In Wisconsin's 1872 tax roll, Patrick and Margaret Coffey owned an 80-acre farm in Waldwick township, valued at $340. They also owned 60 acres in the bordering Moscow township, valued at $380. In 1873, Patrick died at the young age of forty-six. He'd likely died with a sense of pride having acquired so much property after having emigrated with nothing twenty years prior. Three years later when his father, James, died in Ireland, he still leased 30 acres, never having owned the fields he'd worked so hard in his entire life. In 1870, 97 percent of the land was owned by predominantly English landlords, who leased land to tenant farmers. In the following decades a series of laws were passed allowing the Irish to own property. By 1929 97 percent of the land was Irish owned. Unlike his son Patrick in America, James would have no property to pass on to his children except for livestock and farm equipment.

ANCESTRY.COM LIFESTORY

Honestly, I'd never paid much attention to this feature until recently. Now that I've discovered it, I am reading the life stories for everyone in my trees. If you have a family tree on Ancestry.com, check out a person's LifeStory tab. The feature utilizes all the information and documents you've saved to a person's Facts and automatically compiles a story timeline. Here is a tidbit from my Flannery ancestor's LifeStory that just so happened to tie an event in with his name.

> John Francis Flannery lived in Wisconsin during the American Civil War, where everyone eagerly anticipated the day "Johnny" would come marching home again.

INTEGRATE HISTORICAL EVENTS

Knowing what was going on in a country during your ancestor's life is interesting, yet local events really put it in perspective.

> In November 1879, little Margaret Coffey died of diphtheria at the age of nine. In the 1880 mortality schedule, the enumerator noted that the area had been hit hard by the disease, especially children.

> In 1871, the Great Chicago Fire destroyed more than 17,000 wooden buildings. Many Watson and Turney relations emigrated from Ireland and Scotland to work in the family's steam-fitting business to help rebuild Chicago.

PHOTOS ADD A VISUAL STORY

In the next tip, I discuss the importance of preserving family photos and how a photo and postcard provided insight into my great-grandparents' Chicago honeymoon. This enabled me to piece together a terrific story. In addition to photos of people, include ones of places. For example, photos of the house and town your parents or grandparents grew up in. Find a historical photo of your ancestors' homeland circa the time they set sail across the vast ocean to an unknown land.

ANCESTRY RESEARCH IS ABOUT PLACES, NOT MERELY PEOPLE

What gave your ancestors the courage to risk their lives sailing on board a ship for weeks or months in search of a better life? Most of my Irish ancestors emigrated due to the famine. But what brought my dad's Norwegian and German ancestors to America? And why did they choose to settle in southwestern Wisconsin? Had relatives already immigrated to that area, or were they in search of land or employment? In the 1800s several of my ancestors emigrated from a mining area in Ireland to a large lead-mining area in southwestern Wisconsin. Your ancestors' motivations can reveal a lot about their dreams and aspirations.

34

PHOTOS HELP YOU PICTURE
YOUR FAMILY'S HISTORY

I've been known to shed a tear when walking into an antique store or consignment shop and seeing boxes of old photos for sale. How sad that nobody in a family wanted their ancestors' photos, even if their identities were unknown. Yet lack of interest isn't always why pictures end up in shops, or even worse, garbage dumpsters. Years ago my dad's cousin offered him a huge stash of old family photos. When my dad went to pick them up, his cousin was in a surly mood and refused to give him the photos. After his cousin passed away, my dad received a phone call from a lady in his hometown—three hours away—who'd bought his cousin's dresser filled with family photos. Luckily for us, someone who knew my dad's family had purchased the dresser.

My mom and I will spend hours looking through boxes of family photos. A few years ago, I came across a black-and-white one of my great-grandparents Dennis Flannery and Erma Hansen dressed in their finest outfits. The name and address of a Chicago photographer was embossed on the lower corner. Why had the couple traveled several hundred miles from their rural Wisconsin farm to Chicago for a photo shoot? My question was answered when a few minutes later I found a postcard of Chicago's Michigan Avenue, which Erma had sent to her mother. The card's postmark enabled me to date the couple's photo almost to the hour it was taken on November 17, 1916. The couple had been married November 15, 1916, so they were obviously on their honeymoon.

In the card, Erma mentioned that Mrs. Kenney was taking them to have their "mugs shot" later that afternoon before going downtown Chicago for dinner. I knew from research that Mrs. Kenney was formerly Mary Flannery, who in 1910 had lived just a few blocks from the photographer located at 220 Cicero Avenue. Between the postcard, photo, and census, I was able to piece together an interesting story about the couple's honeymoon. I plan to frame the photo and postcard, along with the story. And to think prior to being a genealogist, I would get upset when a photographer "ruined" a photo with his studio information on the front.

An Ancestry.com hint for my Flannery family tree clicked through to what became my only photo of my ancestors James and Mary Flannery, who'd emigrated from Castlebar, County Mayo, Ireland. As if that wasn't a huge enough find, the photo also revealed a clue—the photography studio's name and location in Eldora, Iowa. Traveling a hundred miles from their home in southcentral Wisconsin was quite a distance to have their picture taken. I haven't found evidence that the photographer was a relation they might have been visiting. I Googled the studio and learned that it had operated from the 1860s to the 1880s. Based on the couple's appearance, I estimated the photo was taken in the 1880s. (Knowing a photography studio's name and location is a great way to date a photo.) In the 1880 census, I'd been unable to locate the Flannery family. Was that because they'd moved to Eldora, Iowa? I haven't yet located them in that area, but I'll keep looking. Old photos provide great clues.

When I shared family photos with our Daly relatives in Ireland, they pointed out that my grandma had the Daly chin and nose, as did I. After seeing photos of their grandmother, I totally agreed. I belong to a DNA online group where numerous adoptees who've connected with biological family members post pictures of their newfound relations. The resemblance is often amazing.

Photos offer a peek into your ancestors' everyday lives. Maybe there's a dog in all of your grandpa's photos, confirming he was a dog lover just like you. In almost every early photo of my mom and her siblings, she is holding their hands or has someone sitting in her lap. As the eldest child, she was a caregiver from a young age. When I was young, my grandma Watson was in her sixties, and I remember her wearing handsewn dresses. Photos from her single life in Milwaukee show she'd been quite the fashion diva. She always wrote an outfit's color and fabric on the back of a black-and-white photo. Same as my grandma, I'd been a total clotheshorse in high school. Years ago when my husband and I left a seafood restaurant in a residential area of Milwaukee, I spied a house across the street that I'd seen in many of my grandma's photos. It still had the same shingle siding. The street sign confirmed it was indeed where my grandma had lived.

One picture can literally lead to a thousand words. My grandma Watson gave me a photo of her and a group of girls posing in a city park. They were her coworkers when she lived in Milwaukee before being married and moving back to her small hometown. She shared stories about them going dancing at a place called the Lonely Hearts Club, where the men couldn't refuse a lady's dance request. Once the club's owner was married, he renamed it the Friendship Club. What a great story.

My grandma Watson always had a black-and-white photo on her dresser of herself in her twenties, wearing a chiffon dress and cloche, holding a parasol. Again, fashion diva. When I mentioned how much I loved the photo, she told me the story behind it. She had tagged along with her older sister on the train to a nearby town for a photo shoot. The photographer had asked to take my grandma's photo, even though she told him she had no money to purchase pictures. A few weeks later, she received the proof in the mail. It turned out my favorite photo of my grandma is actually a *proof*. It is framed and sitting on a shelf in my office.

*Dennis and Erma Flannery's honeymoon photo in
Chicago, Illinois, 1916*

The fashionable Grandma Zelda Watson, circa 1927

35

GEDMATCH.COM:

CONNECTING WITH SERIOUS
DNA RESEARCHERS

A DNA test is a great way to collaborate with DNA matches researching the same family lines. *If* the matches you contact reply. I manage seven people's DNA accounts and have about a 25 percent response success rate on Ancestry.com. Why so low when I make sure I am polite, appreciative, and offer to share my tree? Many people don't know their family history, so they don't respond. It's a bit frustrating when you see your message has been read yet no reply. Other members merely wish to discover their ethnicity and never return to their page. Or they dabble in research every few months or years. I recently received a response from a message I sent a year and a half ago. I admire people who have the discipline to walk away from research rather than lose weeks of sleep pulling all-nighters on Ancestry.com. Yet I wouldn't want to be one of them. So how can you increase your chances of connecting with serious researchers? GEDmatch at www.gedmatch.com.

GEDmatch is a third-party online service with applications that compare your DNA results with matches from various testing companies, including Ancestry.com, FamilyTreeDNA, and 23andMe. If a person takes the extra step to download his DNA to

GEDmatch, I find he is usually a more serious researcher than the majority of members on Ancestry.com. Your chance of a response is much greater. The site offers basic to more complex applications. I'm able to navigate the site with my limited knowledge of DNA research.

The only technical term you need to understand for this tip is cM, centiMorgan, which is a unit used to measure genetic distance. You share approximately 3,400 cM with each parent, 850 cM with a first cousin, and 8 cM with a fourth cousin once removed. To learn the genetic distance for more relations, refer to the internet for a cousin-hood chart. Ancestry.com no longer includes DNA matches that share less than 8 cM. They believe a large percentage of matches below this threshold are invalid, and half the valid segments are often twenty generations old. It's hard enough figuring out your relationship to a DNA connection with a common ancestor back five generations. Precisely why you need to test your oldest relative and narrow the gap as much as possible. Yet I've had breakthroughs as a result of 7 cM DNA matches.

Thankfully, GEDmatch has designated 7 cM as the lowest search threshold, or that would eliminate 50 percent of my dad's 20,000 DNA matches on the site. On his paternal side, my dad is a third-generation only child, and his great-grandfather's siblings had no children. This means his closest living match from the Watson line would likely be a third cousin sharing about 53 cM and second-great-grandparents. Most share fewer cM than that. (Maybe I'll luck out and descendants of an unknown male relation back a generation or two will one day show up as a DNA match with my dad.)

GEDmatch offers a nifty tool that compares multiple matches at one time. It's called clustering. This application separates DNA matches into groups that cluster around one of your ancestral lines. Organizing your match list into groups enables you to find the most recent common ancestor (MRCA) that you share with that cluster of people. Once an ancestor or ancestral couple is identified, you can focus your research on that familial line. To use the clustering application, you must subscribe to Tier 1, which is $15 monthly. You could do a one-month subscription and save your results for future reference.

You can create a cluster utilizing your entire database of matches. It will cluster up to five hundred at a time. I requested a fairly narrow threshold for my dad, 20 cM to 500 cM. He has few matches that share more than 50 cM, and if I chose much below 20, he'd have thousands of matches. I want matches on the high end so they'll be more closely related and their relationship to my dad easier to determine. My dad ended up with fifty-nine matches grouped into fourteen clusters, most with five or more matches per cluster. Once I determine the ancestor connected to each cluster, I can decrease the 20 cM to find more distant matches in that cluster. I recently began reaching out to matches in each so that I can determine which ancestor the cluster is related to and separate maternal from paternal matches.

I've also joined several of the hundred GEDmatch Projects with members interested in specific geographic locations, ethnicities, surnames, and niche topics, such as Descendants of Accused Salem Witches. That last one intrigued me, but since I have no known female ancestors living in Salem, Massachusetts, I joined projects for areas and family surnames in Ireland and Scotland. Many projects also have Facebook groups and forums you can join to interact with a large audience of members.

What about all the GEDmatch members who aren't aware that these projects exist? You can take your strongest match from a project and determine your shared matches with that person, then contact them. Projects also help you weed out matches from your other lines. I'm currently researching my dad's paternal line. His mother was supposedly 100 percent Norwegian, so I can figure when I am comparing matches in Ireland and Scotland projects, they are likely from my dad's paternal line. I also can verify this by checking a match against a confirmed paternal match.

The following is an example of how I use the clustering application in my dad's ancestry research to demonstrate the process.

STEP ONE

Establishing a GEDmatch account is free if you don't already have one. This will entail downloading your raw DNA from your test site. Click on Ancestor Projects and select the ones that best meet your needs. It may take up to twenty-four hours for your membership to be confirmed. Joining projects is also free, but don't forget you will need to subscribe to Tier 1 to use the clustering app.

Recently, my dad discovered through an upgraded paternal DNA test that he's biologically a Burke, not a Watson, descended from Richard Óg de Burgh, second Earl of Ulster. (I'm amending the disappointment I voiced in a previous tip over the inconclusive results of my dad's paternal DNA test. It was my fault for not having fully comprehended what the results were trying to tell me. This proves how far I've come with my knowledge of DNA research.) The surname change from Burke to Watson took place sometime in history due to an adoption or other non-paternal event (NPE). The de Burghs had strong ties to Galway, so I joined a County Galway project with 673 members. My dad ended up with few clusters. A DNA match recommended I join the *East* Galway project with 1,942 members, where my dad had many more matches. Don't assume that a project encompassing an entire county or country will have more participants. Many researchers want to narrow the field as much as possible.

STEP TWO

Select one of your projects. I'll choose my dad's Argyllshire, Scotland, project for this example. Decide on the number of cM for the lower and upper thresholds. DNA matches have helped me account for the females in my dad's paternal line back five generations. Thus, the

Burke to Watson surname change occurred prior to that time. This means I'm looking for distant relations, so I need to use a lower threshold than when I did clusters for the entire database of matches. Despite Ancestry.com's advice not to go below 8 cM, I choose a lower threshold of 7 cM and an upper one of 50 cM. I also request the report to note the number of generations back to the matches and my dad's most common recent ancestor. I click the button, and the program goes to work comparing my dad's kit to 605 project participants. In under a minute, the report appears.

STEP THREE

With a lower threshold of 7 cM and upper one of 50 cM, my dad has about fifty matches out of the 605 participants. Why so few? Many of the Argyllshire project members were likely not a DNA match, and those who share less than 7 cM weren't included. My dad has seven matches who share the most common related ancestor back 5.2 to 6 generations—the rest are 6 to 7.5 generations. I have found that an estimated 6 to 7.5 generations could actually turn out to be 10 generations. The less DNA shared, the more difficult it is to estimate a relationship. The report has a tree icon next to members who've supplied a tree on GEDmatch or Wiki. About 5 percent of my dad's matches have a tree, and many names are hidden. Why so few? Maybe members want to be contacted directly. The report also provides email addresses. I print the report, then click the button to start the clustering program.

STEP FOUR

Colorful square clusters appear on a grid with the matches' names and their shared amount of cM down the left-hand side. My dad has six randomly colored clusters ranging from two to twenty matches in a cluster. Those names in the green cluster share a common ancestor, those in pink another common relation, and so on. Clusters can be displayed in various ways, such as by those with the highest average cM, cluster size, and more. Now that you have these lovely clusters, what do you do with them?

STEP FIVE

Contact matches to determine your relationship and ancestor connection. I put the project name in the subject so the person immediately knows the purpose of my email. I keep the information brief and concise. I introduce myself as the manager of my dad's account, with whom they are a match. I'll include *possible* surname connections for their shared cluster. I ask if they might be kind enough to share a tree if they have one, and I offer to share my dad's. I paste the line from the GEDmatch report illustrating the person and my dad's connection. Then I anxiously wait for responses, which arrive within minutes, weeks, or never. I've had about a 60 percent response success rate from project matches. After two weeks I resend the email to nonrespondents in case it's sitting in their spam boxes. I'll switch the subject and eliminate attachments in case either item flagged the previous email as spam.

STEP SIX

I track all responses in an Excel database, including the match's profile name, the project name, cluster color, ancestors' surnames and locations, email address, and notes. It often takes an hour to analyze a person's tree if he provided one. When you're tracing back five or more generations, there could be several possible connections with a person.

If you've taken a DNA test, I highly recommend giving clustering a go. There are also numerous YouTube videos on the subject.

MILITARY RECORDS:

INSIGHT INTO YOUR ANCESTOR'S LIFE AND ROLE IN HISTORICAL EVENTS

My high school history teacher would be proud of me for writing this tip about military documents. I struggled to make good grades in a class about memorizing dates, names, battles, and wars, many of which took place hundreds of years ago on the other side of the world. I couldn't have cared less about what some dead French guy did in the 1800s. When you're a kid, you're focused on the present and future, not what happened before you were born. Besides finding the subject matter boring, I was hopeless when it came to remembering dates and names. Or so I'd thought, until I began conducting genealogical research.

I amaze my mother, and myself, when we go on our annual cemetery visits to put flowers on our relatives' graves. I can rattle off the dates our ancestors emigrated, their birth location, parents' names, and probably pets' names if I knew them. Suddenly I can relate to the Civil War because several of my Irish ancestors had emigrated merely a few years prior to it. After surviving the hardships of the Great Famine, they fought for a country in which they hadn't yet obtained citizenship. If high school history classes encouraged ancestry research, maybe uninterested students would become more involved, knowing their families' connections to historical events.

My *possible* Scottish ancestor John Watson enlisted in the Donegal Regiment to protect Ireland when things were heating up at the advent of the Napoleonic Wars. How cool to have had a relative who was prepared to defend Ireland against that French guy I never cared about. Unexpectedly I found myself reading scholastic papers written by military experts. I'll never forget that the Napoleonic Wars took place from 1803 to 1815, and my ancestor had fought in the famous battle at Waterloo. A battle which even *I* was familiar with.

Wanting to learn about the Donegal Regiment, I contacted the Letterkenny Historical Society in County Donegal. A helpful gentleman sent me an article he'd authored on the regiment and informed me that the National Library of Ireland holds the regiment's rosters for 1801 to 1811 and 1825 to 1852. They also have correspondence written by the regiment's top officers. And what about the Letterkenny Garrison? Was it still there? Could I visit it on my next trip to Ireland?

I actually wanted to vacation in County Donegal to visit a military garrison rather than walk along the beaches on scenic Achill Island. Growing up, my father dragged us kids to history museums on vacation. It would be an all-day event because he had to read every word, on every plaque, in every exhibit. We kids would spend an hour in the dinosaur exhibit, then head to the cafeteria. Lunch out was the highlight of our visit. Now, I couldn't wait to get my hands on a copy of these military papers. Even if my ancestor wasn't mentioned in them, they would provide insight into a soldier's life at that time. And the rosters would confirm when John had joined the military and might include other family surnames, providing more leads.

Military discharge papers provided background on my James Watson, who immigrated to Canada. His children's baptismal records in Montreal noted that he was a soldier in Her Majesty's 23rd

Regiment Fusiliers. I hired a genealogist to retrieve James's military discharge papers from the UK's archives. (These papers are now indexed on Ancestry.com. If you have an all access Ancestry.com membership, you can view the original document. If you don't, you can view the record for a nominal fee online at Fold3, a site which specializes in military records.) I learned James was born in 1811 in Pollokshaws, Scotland. The papers tracked his entire military career from Scotland to County Down, Ireland, to Canada, listing every regiment, transfer, and promotion.

James Watson Jr.'s death certificate incorrectly stated that he was born in Kingston, Ontario, Canada, which is actually where he'd grown up. This is another reason why military records are a great resource. The information is usually provided by the *living* ancestor himself. In the *Historical Register of US National Homes for Disabled Volunteer Soldiers 1866–1938* on Ancestry.com, I found two admittance records for James, both having Montreal as his birthplace. The document also included detailed personal and military information, such as he'd enlisted in the Civil War in Albany, New York. Since he'd lived in Canada, I would never even have thought of him having fought in that war. Remember, my fascination with history is fairly recent.

All this success led me to check military records for my ancestor John Turney, also living in Kingston, Ontario. In Canada's *British Regimental Registers of Service*, I found an enlistment record for a John Turney born in 1790 in Ballinderry, County Antrim, Northern Ireland. This was close to my ancestor's birth date, and Turney was an uncommon name. Yet I wasn't sure this was my John. I later had several DNA matches whose Turney ancestors had lived twenty miles from Ballinderry. Interesting.

Since the Irish and Scottish loved their drink, I searched the *Military Courts Martial Registers* for more records of John Turney serving in Canada. In 1841 a John Turney was tried for drunkenness in Montreal. I'm not certain that's my John, since mine had been married in Kingston, Ontario, five years earlier. But once again, Turney was an uncommon surname. In 1845 a John Turney was tried in Kingston, Ontario. I'm fairly confident this was my John. His criminal charges helped me track the family's movement and will hopefully assist with locating his children's baptismal records, which aren't online and apparently still stashed away in a Canadian church's archives.

I mentioned this in a previous tip, but it's worth repeating. The paper trail in Chicago for my ancestor James William Watson (James IV) vanished after his WWI draft card. Later I discovered a WWII draft card for a William James Watson with the same birth date. It turned out James had switched his middle and first names following a divorce, possibly to elude family financial obligations. If I hadn't known James's middle name, I never would have checked a document for a William James. I've obtained numerous middle names from WWI and WWII draft cards. Middle names have helped me piece together ancestry trees based on the traditional Irish naming pattern. The records are also a great resource for occupation, address, birth location and date, and a relative's contact information.

I have located Civil War discharge records for several ancestors but none of their pension or widow's pension records. A pension file can be a gold mine of information for a time period when historical records are scarce. A person's pension application may include his military rank, unit, period of service, residence, age, date and place of birth and marriage, wife's maiden name, and the nature of a disability. To provide evidence of his service, he may have included documents such as discharge papers or affidavits from fellow soldiers. Widows or heirs had to prove their relationship to the veteran, supplying marriage records and other documents. The file may list the names of dependent children under the age of sixteen. The index for the widow's pension is a great resource for finding the husband's death date.

Wow! I have spent years searching for the amount of information often included in this single military file. A Civil War pension index is available at Ancestry.com and FamilySearch. The actual pension records are currently only available through the National Archives and Records Administration in Washington, DC. Even though I haven't found these records for my ancestors, I will continue looking. Once again, genealogical research is all about perseverance.

37

INQUIRING MINDS WANT TO KNOW: AUTHOR Q&A

WHAT DOES IT TAKE TO BECOME A SUCCESSFUL GENEALOGIST?

The five Ps.

Perseverance

You will undoubtedly encounter many setbacks while researching your ancestors. You need to be able to brush it off and move on.

Patience

Don't expect to walk into an archive and out with a family tree. Or that you'll find an accurate, completed tree already online. Ancestry research takes time, lots of time.

Problem-Solving Skills

Clues and leads often don't scream out at you from a document. You need to be able to analyze and evaluate vague, confusing, and conflicting information.

Poirot

Like Agatha Christie's fictional private detective Hercule Poirot, you must love to solve mysteries. Curiosity is what will keep you up until 4:00 a.m. following a new lead and motivate you to find answers.

Passion

To me, this is the most critical P. You can have perseverance, patience, problem-solving skills, and Poirot's inquisitiveness, but none of that matters if you don't have passion for genealogy.

HOW DO YOU BEGIN A NEW RESEARCH PROJECT?

By sitting at my computer having a panic attack. The *lack* of information I usually have when starting to research a new line is overwhelming. All I knew about my ancestor Patrick Coffey was that his tombstone claimed he was born in Ireland in 1825 and died in Wisconsin in 1873. I had no clue where to begin. You can read about it in my Coffey Family Case Study. I have never approached research the same way twice. It all depends on what information I have to start with.

Actually, that's not completely true. The first thing I do is see if there is a family tree online. I've never been lucky enough to find a detailed tree for any of my lines. However, I have found several for family and friends. I still spend time verifying the accuracy of the information. And not by merely checking it against other trees, which is quite possibly where the tree obtained the wrong information from in the first place. And a tree including ten thousand people may provide less pertinent and correct information than a three-hundred-person tree. With a tree that extensive, it's often impossible to determine which people the tree's owner is actually related to since many people include potential relations that are pending verification.

HOW MUCH MONEY HAVE YOU SPENT ON RESEARCH?

I will never admit how much money I have spent on research. I don't want to scare people off from researching because nowadays there are much more economical means of obtaining genealogical information. I began ancestry research thirteen years ago when less information was available online. I've had to hire numerous genealogists to research documents in archives and churches. Tracing my Coffey line entailed going down many wrong paths and purchasing incorrect records before finding the correct ones. I paid a genealogist $250 to retrieve my Watson ancestor's military record from the UK archives, now free with an all access Ancestry.com subscription or on Fold3 for a nominal fee. Thankfully, the record provided a wealth of information, which isn't always the case.

HOW MANY FAMILY LINES HAVE YOU TRACED?

I've researched twenty-five of my maternal and paternal Irish and Scottish lines. I've also assisted numerous family members and friends with research in England, Hungary, and Austria.

HOW MANY HOURS HAVE YOU PUT INTO RESEARCH?

Thousands, and thousands, and thousands . . . I've been known to go to bed at 4:00 a.m. when my husband is getting up for work. Besides conducting online research, I've made dozens of trips to archives and cemeteries in Chicago and southwestern Wisconsin. I've also spent a fair amount of time in Ireland's cemeteries searching for ancestors, and in pubs hoping to stumble upon a living relative with whom I can enjoy a pint.

HAVE YOU EVER DISCOVERED INFORMATION THAT YOU'VE KEPT A SECRET?

My family is quite open minded and not easily shocked, so I've shared most everything with them. For example, the background information and testimony included in divorce papers often explain how neglect, abuse, or alcoholism affected family members. Knowing what shaped a person can help you and loved ones better understand their actions. I also feel that people deserve to know the truth. Most people are several generations removed from what I discover, so anything negative really wouldn't upset them.

WHAT WAS YOUR MOST EXCITING DISCOVERY?

At the top would be my father's paternal DNA test revealing that he is biologically a Burke rather than a Watson, descended from Richard Óg de Burgh, second Earl of Ulster and Richard the Lionheart, king of England. Second, when I located my ancestor Patrick Coffey's naturalization record and learned he had emigrated from County Westmeath, Ireland, in 1851. I'd been at a brick wall for months when I'd found this tissue-paper-thin document at an archive in southwestern Wisconsin. Third would be finding James Watson's military discharge papers that noted his birth location as Pollok-shaws, Scotland. This enabled my family to visit his hometown and narrowed the scope of my research.

WHAT IS THE ONE THING YOU'D MOST LIKE TO DISCOVER?

At what point and where our paternal line surname changed from Burke to Watson and what caused the change. I'm hoping the discovery will be the material movies or best-selling novels are based on.

WHY DON'T YOU BECOME A PROFESSIONAL GENEALOGIST IF YOU ENJOY IT SO MUCH?

I already don't get enough sleep. It doesn't matter if I'm researching my own family line or someone else's, I become obsessed with solving the genealogical mystery. Also, I could never charge for all the actual hours I work. Clients would never believe it when I submit an invoice for a hundred-hour workweek.

YOU WRITE TWO GENEALOGY-THEMED FICTION SERIES. WHICH CAME FIRST, YOUR PASSION FOR WRITING OR GENEALOGICAL RESEARCH?

I began my writing career in 2000 when I attended my first romance writers conference. That was seven years prior to discovering my passion for genealogy. I'm fortunate to be able to combine my greatest passions in life.

BESIDES FINDING MANY DEAD RELLIES, HAVE YOU FOUND LIVING ONES?

Yes, you can read all about them in Tip 48, "Tracing Your Family Backward and Then Forward to Find Living Relatives."

DO YOUR HUSBAND AND FAMILY UNDERSTAND YOUR OBSESSION WITH CEMETERIES AND DEAD PEOPLE?

I'm not sure if they fully understand it, but they accept it. Several family members have an interest in genealogy and our Irish heritage, so they appreciate the amount of time and effort I've put into it. Learning about our ancestors has led us on some interesting adventures in Ireland and Scotland. People might sometimes get a bit tired of visiting more cemeteries than tourist attractions, but they are great sports.

38

ELIZA WATSON OR MACWATTIE?

TRACING ANCESTORS WITH SURNAME VARIATIONS, CHANGES, AND ALIASES

My dad's paternal DNA test resulted in no Watson matches, and 50 percent had the Burke surname in various forms—Burke, Bourke, Birk—which turned out to be my dad's biological surname. The other matches' last names either went back to the time of pre-standardized surnames or, like our Watson line, were a result of an NPE causing a surname change due to an adoption, an illegitimate birth and the child is given the mother's surname, or for other various reasons.

China had the first recorded surnames dating back to 2852 BC. Ireland was one of the first, if not the first, places in Europe to adopt hereditary surnames, with O'Clery (Ó Cléirigh) being the earliest documented one in County Galway in AD 916. After 1066 the Norman invasion introduced surnames into England, and eventually they were passed on. By 1400 most of England and lowland Scotland were using hereditary surnames. Surnames were often derived from a person's profession, place of origin, and father's name. Brewster comes from the occupation of a brewer and Smith from a blacksmith. Leonardo da Vinci's name was derived from his hometown, "Leonard from Vinci."

In Ireland almost all surnames were patronymic, using Mc or Mac "son of" or O' "grandson of." Despite common belief that the prefix Mc is Irish and Mac is Scottish, both can be either. In the 1600s, when English rule intensified in Ireland, the prefixes O' and Mc/Mac were often dropped to avoid increased discrimination for having an Irish-sounding name. In the late 1800s, Irish land wars against English landlords inspired families to add the prefixes back to their names. Sometimes the wrong prefix was adopted, changing the name. Once MacDonnell, the name might now be O'Donnell. They were just trying to keep genealogists on their toes. After Irish Independence in 1922, the reclamation of O' and Mc/Mac increased dramatically.

The Norwegian naming pattern was largely patronymic, but some preferred to use the name of the family farmstead as a last name. Thankfully, my grandma Watson's Norwegian ancestry was well documented. Researching the patronymic naming pattern, which changed with each generation until the late 1800s, would have been challenging. By 1923 the Norwegian government mandated that families choose a standardized surname to be passed down generation to generation. Prior to this the most common last names in Norway ended in -son, -sen, -dotter, or -datter, which mean "son of" or "daughter of." My ancestor Siri Jensdatter would have been the daughter of Jens. The one benefit would be knowing her dad's first name. It appears my third-great-grandfather was torn about whether to use his father's or their farm's name, so he used both. Ole Johansen Wahler, son of Johan living on the Wahler farm.

When you start researching an ancestor, be aware of all the possible surname variations. Watson has been recorded as Wattson, Walterson, MacWattie, Wattessone, and many others. I have to say MacWattie would make a cute nickname. Imagine a genealogist one day trying to determine if MacWattie and Elizabeth Watson were the same person. My Kerr relations were often spelled Karr or Carr. Kerr is phonetically pronounced Karr, so either people recorded it as it sounded or my ancestors became tired of their name being misspelled so they changed it. Also keep in mind that many people couldn't write their own name and relied on others to determine the spelling.

Sometimes people changed surnames throughout history. For example, a Scottish person with the surname Mackenzie probably believes he's a member of Clan Mackenzie. However, he might take a Y-DNA paternal test and discover he's biologically a Bonar. People often became affiliated with a clan for protection or to work for clan leaders and adopted its surname to show solidarity.

People also took on aliases. I was helping a friend research her English ancestor Richard Coleman. We came across an English marriage record for a Richard *Irish* and a Margaret Coleman. In addition to the family name Coleman, both their fathers' first names and the marriage date matched my friend's ancestors. It appeared that after being married, the couple immigrated to America and changed their last name Irish to the woman's maiden name Coleman. This was in the mid-1800s at the height of Irish emigration due to the famine. In America many storefront signs read No Irish Need Apply. My guess would be Richard didn't want his surname *Irish* being mistaken for the ethnicity and causing him to endure discrimination when he was English. It was easy to change your identity back when documentation was scarce, making it nearly impossible to track people.

Here is one of the more intriguing scenarios I've encountered with name aliases. My dad has numerous DNA matches associated with the name MaGee/McKee. Yet we have no known ancestors with this name. After analyzing many of the matches, I discovered several are descended from a MaGee family in Virginia. When reviewing their trees and tracing the line back, I learned that the surname went from MaGee in 1742, to McGehee in 1702, to MackGehee in 1672, to MackGayhe in 1618 back in Scotland. Eventually I discovered the family's surname originally wasn't a variation of any of these MaGee names. It was MacGregor.

It turns out that William MackGayhe born 1618 in Scotland was actually James MacGregor of Clan Gregor/MacGregor. He changed his name and fled to America to avoid English persecution. His clan's troubles in Scotland began in the thirteenth century when King Robert the Bruce of Scotland gave a section of Clan MacGregor's land to the bordering Clan Campbell. This fueled a clan feud that spanned centuries and often put the MacGregors on the opposite side of the law, eventually pushing them deeper into the Scottish Highlands. They became known as Children of the Mist. In 1603 King James VI decreed the name MacGregor be abolished following the murder of the King's Forester, killed for hanging several MacGregor clansmen for poaching. All who bore the name had to renounce it or die. Anyone answering to the name was executed on the spot, with women and children sold into slavery in the American states. There were no legal ramifications for outright killing a MacGregor. How horrible was that?

Not only does my dad have numerous DNA matches with MaGee in all its many forms but many matches with Gregory/Gregor/McGregor/MacGregor. And besides MaGee, one of Clan MacGregor's known surname aliases was Grieve. I discuss how I'd connected this surname to our family in Tip 28, "Was She Mary, Molly, or Polly? Identifying Unusual Nicknames." Also remember, a paternal DNA test revealed that my family surname changed from Burke to Watson at some point in history. Maybe a male Burke became a MacGregor in the 1400s and then a descendant became a Watson in the 1600s to avoid persecution. Who knows what the connection will turn out to be? As if it's not challenging enough tracing *one* surname, I might now be tracing a dozen aliases.

Yet sometimes there is no apparent reason for a name change. We have connections to the name Love in Northern Ireland. When I was searching for a Barbara Neil in Scotland, I found one born circa my Barbara's birth date to a Matthew Neil and Mary *Dove*. Could Love once have been Dove? My dad has a DNA match whose tree has a man named Love with a son named Dove, which stuck with future generations. What caused the change? Had they been eluding the law? Had it been recorded wrong in the baptismal register and they'd decided to go with it?

One can only speculate the reasons behind name changes. Bottom line, go with your gut and keep an open mind when you come across possible surname variations. Even though historical records may be written in black and white, as a genealogist you need to be able to decipher their many degrees of gray.

39

FAMILY REUNIONS:

MORE THAN POTLUCK AND PLAYING CARDS

Holding a family reunion is not merely a great way to stay in touch with family members you rarely see—it's a chance to meet new relations. When I discovered that my Flannery ancestor emigrated from Ireland to Wisconsin with his parents and four brothers, I placed an ad in his hometown-area newspapers inviting his brothers' descendants to the reunion. Several unknown local relations, and even a couple from Maryland, attended. The ad provided my email address, so several people contacted me in advance. I asked each of the newfound relatives to complete an ancestry tree so we could learn how they fit into the family line. I also suggested that they bring copies of family photos or email them to me so I could display them on a picture board.

A gathering is the perfect opportunity to bring out family photos and try to determine unidentified relatives. I regret not having my older relatives record people's names, even if it was with an ink pen on the front of the photo, like many of our vintage ones. Yet even photos with nameless relations are a treasured part of our collection and can make great conversation. I shared copies of my favorites with guests. Also, what better time to pass along your photos of loved ones no longer with you to their immediate family members?

While I was talking with a great-uncle at the reunion, he offered to drive my mom and me around the area to view old family homes. He showed us the rural neighboring homes where my grandma Coffey and grandpa Flannery had lived and first met. He shared stories about why the family moved to various locations. He pointed out the spot where my grandma's young cousin and his dog were struck by lightning and killed while sitting under a tree. This explained my grandma's fear of thunderstorms. I remember her reciting the rosary and burning palm leaves during wicked storms. Before I heard this story, her fear had seemed irrational.

In another tip, I recommended a list of questions to ask your older relatives. You could send the list to them in advance and ask them to complete it prior to the reunion. However, it might not be completed in its entirety or to your satisfaction. I would ask relatives to answer the questions before or following the gathering so you don't infringe on their visiting time with family members. Rather than writing down their answers, ask if you can record them. This will expedite the Q&A process and give you an oral account of stories prompted by the questions.

Have a family history corner offering photocopies of ancestor biographies, family trees, and picture boards. We also put together photo albums noting relatives' names, which sparked people's memories of the persons or the occasions, even some family folklore.

Request donations so you are reimbursed for photocopied items, invite mailings, and other reunion supplies. I don't expect to ever recoup the amount I've spent on research, but funds for the event are appreciated.

Have a potluck asking people to bring a favorite dish or dessert that has been passed down in the family. Following the meal is an ideal time for family traditions, such as playing a game of Euchre—a popular card game in southwestern Wisconsin. Have people stand up and introduce themselves and explain their family relation. Maybe a few will volunteer to share a short family story.

Before people leave, plan the next reunion. Have newfound relations provide their addresses for future invites. Ask people to volunteer for roles, such as creating and mailing invitations, printing photos, and assisting with a bit of research to get them more involved. Urge people to commit while their interest is piqued. Encourage them to reach out to you with information prior to the next reunion. Keep the interest and momentum going down through the generations!

40

TRUTH OR DARE:

ARE YOU PREPARED FOR YOUR
DNA RESULTS?

What if you take a DNA test and discover you and your brother have no matches in common? However, he has matches with all your known relations. Shocked, you come to the conclusion you were adopted. You confront your parents, who deny your adoption, showing you photos of your mother's pregnancy a month before you were born. Now you are all baffled. Upon a closer look at your DNA matches, you discover two biological siblings. You reach out to them and learn you were born the day after their sister, in the same hospital. It turns out their sister and you were switched at birth. Are you happy about learning the truth, or would you have preferred to remain clueless and go on with life as you knew it?

I know several people whose DNA test results revealed this exact scenario and also ones who discovered they were adopted or that a parent isn't their biological one. I had a positive experience connecting with a cousin who'd been given up for adoption many years ago. And my dad's paternal Y-DNA test revealing he isn't biologically a Watson, but rather a Burke with royal lineage, has been one of my most interesting discoveries. But not all surprises might be good. Before you decide to take a test, be sure you are prepared to accept whatever you might learn.

My dad and his closest paternal Y-DNA match have a shared common ancestor, who lived circa 1600. I have confirmed my dad's paternal line back five generations through DNA matches, so I was excited at the prospect of this match possibly allowing me to trace back further. I contacted the man's daughter, who manages his account. We exchanged a half dozen emails, yet she was still baffled that our fathers were biologically Burkes. After all, her documented family history *confirmed* she was descended from a prestigious English line. She said, "Are you suggesting our last name isn't Crowley? My ancestors came over on the Mayflower, so any name change had to have occurred prior to 1620. I *guarantee* it didn't happen in the past five generations." I don't believe that's a *guarantee* a person can make even back *one* generation. Many male surname changes occurred due to infidelity, adoptions, and other family secrets. Sadly, I thought it best to stop communicating with her rather than assuring her that DNA doesn't lie. Her reaction demonstrated that many people are not prepared for the outcome of DNA tests.

When I was perusing a jail register in a county courthouse in my ancestor's hometown, I came across his name. Expecting a drunk and disorderly or a petty charge, I was quite shocked to find a woman had charged my married ancestor with sexual solicitation. A few months later, she filed a paternity suit demanding child support. Good to know. I'm now prepared should a descendant of this child one day appear as a DNA match. Even if I'm not as well prepared for other DNA surprises, I will remain open minded and go where the DNA leads me.

41

HOW TO MAKE THE MOST OF AN ANCESTRY.COM ACCOUNT

Establishing an Ancestry.com account is free. Viewing DNA matches, creating family trees, and posting to message boards don't require a paid subscription. However, searching the site's billions of historical records does. You can take advantage of a fourteen-day free trial to help you decide if you want to take the plunge and sign up for at least a monthly subscription. If you aren't convinced about the benefits of being a member, check out their Ancestry Academy. There are dozens of free videos on topics from navigating the site to researching specific records and analyzing DNA results. The following are a few of my favorite aspects of this site.

The message boards don't require a subscription, and I've used them since I began genealogical research thirteen years ago. These are different from the private messaging system that enables you to contact members. There are hundreds, maybe thousands, of message boards categorized by geographical locations or topics, such as census and cemeteries. For locale, a country like Canada is divided into provinces and then by counties. You can search by a surname or keywords to see if anyone has posted about your area of interest. If not, you can start a new thread. I've connected with people researching the same family lines and even had unrelated members offer to assist me with obtaining gravestone photos and historical records. My posts from thirteen years ago are still active, and once in a while someone will reach out to me. Many forums come and go, but I believe these will be around for generations.

Of course, creating family trees on the site are great for organizing the wealth of information you'll discover about your ancestors. Besides including relations in my trees, I also track possible connections. However, I don't link them to a particular person in the tree until I have confirmed their relation. Once I narrowed down Bridget Connolly's family in Montreal, Canada, to two families, I added them to her tree. Even though none of the potential relatives' pages were physically linked to Bridget's, a ThruLines hint suggested she was descended from the Connollys in County Tipperary. ThruLines is a feature that illustrates how you *might* be connected to a particular DNA match through a common ancestor. I evaluated the hint but haven't confirmed the family connection.

When someone makes a correction to one of your ancestor's historical records, reach out to the person. Recently I was reviewing a Social Security record I'd saved to my great-grandfather James Watson's page. I noticed that six months ago a member had noted a correction. My father has no known living Watson relations, so my interest is piqued when someone saves a Watson record to a tree, especially when that person has enough family knowledge to realize there was an error. I excitedly checked out the member's profile page and discovered that her family was attempting to learn the cause behind a relative's disappearance after emigrating from Glasgow, Scotland, to Ontario, Canada, in the early 1900s. My ancestor James Watson Sr. had emigrated from Glasgow to Ontario in the mid-1800s. Believing there must be a family connection, I reached out to her. Hopefully, she'll respond.

Four of the five photos I have of my ancestors who emigrated from Ireland have come from trees on Ancestry.com. I always reach out and thank members for sharing photos and helpful information.

This also provides an opportunity to learn their family connection and possibly collaborate on research. It's always a bonus if the person knows the story behind the photo. Every photo has one.

I'm forever warning people about the danger of assuming an online family tree is accurate. More than 50 percent of the time I find errors. Well, sometimes it turns out that even incorrect information in a tree can be helpful as long as you *know* it's not correct. I came across a Coffey family tree that included the wrong parents. The couple's first names were correct, and the death dates were close, but our Coffey couple hadn't immigrated to America. I have copies of their Irish death certificates and know a descendant of theirs in Ireland. Yet the similarities between the couples intrigued me. Merely a coincidence or a possible connection? One more lead to follow.

Ancestry.com has that cool feature I mentioned earlier called LifeStory. This program takes the dates, records, and relationships that you've attached to a person in your tree, along with historical events from the time and place they lived, and auto-generates a story. I love a tidbit that appeared as part of my ancestor James Watson's story. James had emigrated from Scotland to Canada as part of Her Majesty's Military and retired in Kingston, Ontario, in 1856. Four years later Prince Albert visited the city. A black-and-white photo of the military event enabled me to clearly envision James as a spectator at this celebration honoring the prince. LifeStory often provides interesting bits to add to a family biography.

*Patrick Daly (1858–1935) from
Kilbeggan, County Westmeath, Ireland*

*Patrick Coffey's sister Mary (1830–1895) from
County Westmeath, Ireland*

HELLO, IS ANYONE OUT THERE?

HOW TO RECEIVE RESPONSES FROM DNA OR FAMILY TREE MATCHES

I'm lucky if 25 percent of the people I reach out to on Ancestry.com respond. It's a bit frustrating. On a rare occasion, I've chosen not to reply to a message if the person came across rude or demanding. I check my Ancestry.com inbox every few weeks just in case I've forgotten to reply to a message or the system failed to notify me of one. I know how it feels to be on the *non*-receiving end. Even if I'm unable to provide the requested information, it takes two minutes to write, *Sorry. I've got nothing.* I receive one new message every month or two. It's not as if I'm overwhelmed by them, so I can't imagine that it's any different for other members. I understand things happen that prevent people from responding, but 75 percent of them?

What have I done to ease my obvious frustration and increase my chances of a response? First off, don't set yourself up for disappointment. Weed out those less likely to respond. If the person doesn't have a tree attached to an account, he possibly doesn't have much family history knowledge or doesn't care to share it. My response success rate for people willing to share private trees has been fairly good.

Why do people have private rather than public trees? My trees are private because they contain unverified information that I don't want others adding to their trees. Once while searching for my ancestors in other members' trees, I came across a tree identical to mine, except that my unverified information showed as valid. Tracing my trees back to the 1700s has taken me a lot of time and money. I was a bit miffed that this person copied my hard work without even a thank-you. Besides having created trees to organize my research, I'd hoped to connect with other family historians. I messaged the person and tactfully reminded her that much of the information was pending verification. No response. I'm sorry, but there is a code of ethics and conduct for genealogists.

If a person created an account in February 2020 and hasn't signed in since March, and it's now December, he's likely gone MIA. Many people take a DNA test merely to learn their ethnicity, and others sometimes discover shocking news they regret uncovering. Rather than deleting or hiding their account, they ignore it. Their profile generally doesn't contain any identifying information, not even their general location or last name. They likely appear unapproachable because they wish to remain private. Or if they haven't signed on in over a year, they might have passed away. Genealogy is a popular hobby with the elderly population.

Many adoptees take DNA tests in search of their biological parents. I've helped several. If a person doesn't know the identity of a parent or sibling, the thought of trying to determine a second-cousin connection is undoubtedly overwhelming. Even if someone isn't adopted, many people are unable to name relations back further than their grandparents. Before embarking on my genealogy journey, I bet I could only name two of my eight great-grandparents. My grandpa Watson never had a relationship with his father, so Grandpa was the only Watson I ever knew. The more distantly related a match, the less likely you'll receive a response.

If you decide to reach out to someone, how can you increase your chance of a response? Be specific in your subject line. *We're second cousins on my Watson side.* If you've reviewed a person's tree, explain your possible connection, thank him for sharing the tree, and mention any photo or tidbit of information you found helpful. Offer to reciprocate in any way you can.

If you are in a rush when typing up the message, make sure you aren't abrupt, or you may come off as impolite and demanding. I recently received a one-line message. *Yeah, what can you tell me about your Watson ancestors?* No *please* or *thank you.* Besides sounding rude, could he have been more vague? What about my Watsons? I have several binders on the Watson family line. If he'd at least been polite, I'd have responded, inquiring about *what* exactly he wanted to know.

Hook them with the first sentence. Let people know if you have a ticking timeline. *I am helping a ninety-eight-year-old English woman search for her paternal grandfather . . .* With the lack of responses I receive, unless this woman miraculously lives another twenty years, I have no hope of finding her answers. So that's now the opening line in my messages when contacting her matches. Who doesn't want to help an elderly lady discover her paternal line? Or how about, *I was shocked to learn my father isn't biologically a Watson and is descended from royalty.* The person on the receiving end is immediately engaged. I can almost hear her excited gasp as her mind races, wondering if she shares my royal lineage.

Update your résumé. Make sure your profile includes at least some identifying information. A blank profile screams to be left alone. Someone is much more likely to reach out to you if there appears to be a live person on the receiving end. If you have a vague profile name like ANC126593GEN, consider changing it to at least a first initial and last name. Provide the surnames and locations you're researching. An age range is extremely helpful when I'm comparing DNA to estimate the person's generation. I show I'm a team player by offering to assist others researching the same family lines. I'm enthusiastic and determined, stating that I research daily.

Show them your pearly whites. Until recently my profile picture was Ancestry.com's faceless woman's pink profile. I blended in with millions of other women on the site. I realized this one morning at 3:00 a.m. when I was reviewing my dad's shared DNA matches. A smiling lady's face kept popping up, keeping me company in the wee hours of the morning. I'd smile back and think, *Well, hello again, Linda.* The fact that her family tree shared numerous surnames with my dad's turned out to be a major clue. If she'd had the generic pink woman's profile pic, she likely wouldn't have stood out, and her connection wouldn't have clicked with my tired brain. I felt a bond with someone I didn't even know. I have updated the profile pictures on my parents' and my sites with our travels in Ireland. We look like the type of fun and friendly rellies you would enjoy hanging out with in a pub. Even a fourth cousin twice removed will be eager to learn our connection. Fingers crossed anyway!

43

TEN THINGS I WISH
I HAD DONE DIFFERENTLY

1. WALKED AWAY FROM A BRICK WALL RATHER THAN BEATING MY HEAD AGAINST IT

Genealogy is a hobby, not a full-time job for most people. Making the best use of your time often means walking away from a brick wall and returning to the research a week or a month later with a clear mind. Or even a year later when more information has become available that might provide the needed breakthrough. Sadly, sometimes you must come to terms with the fact that you might never find the needed information because it might never have existed or no longer exists. Like my Patrick Coffey's Irish baptismal record.

2. CONDUCTED RESEARCH IN PERSON

I could have driven to Kingston, Ontario, Canada, and spent a week at a hotel for the amount of money I've paid others to locate historical documents. The same is true with Ireland and Scotland. Of course, when I embark on an area of research, I have no idea the amount of time or money that will ultimately be spent on it. It's also difficult to pass along all the random knowledge in my brain to someone else. When I'm reading through a document, a surname or place I came across five months ago often jumps out at me. In-person research would also have given me the opportunity to spend time uncovering hidden treasures at historical societies and archives. And who knows what clues might have come up in a conversation with local experts. I also could have visited my ancestors' graves and crossed one more cemetery off my bucket list.

3. LISTENED TO MY INSTINCTS SOONER

Lack of experience can cause you to question your instincts. I finally listened to a nagging feeling that I was heading down the wrong path searching for a marriage record in Ireland despite a genealogist's failed attempt to locate one in Canada. A week prior to a family trip to Ireland, I had him double-check his research, and his second attempt proved successful, at no charge. He'd originally overlooked my ancestors' misspelled names. I've done the same thing myself numerous times. If not misspelled, faded records with poor penmanship can be difficult to read. Yet the discovery had come too late to pursue before the trip.

You also need to listen to your instincts when deciding if a research find is merely coincidence or fact. I've had to make that determination dozens of times. This is a difficult decision because the wrong one could lead you down an incorrect path for months or even years. But even a wrong path is often better than no path and sitting idle on information.

4. ORGANIZED MY RESEARCH

Funny that this was an issue, since most of my professional career has been spent as an event planner, which requires superior organizational skills. Early on in my research, I was tracing ten Irish lines at once. I had a lot of all-night sessions on Ancestry.com and was tossing my finds into piles on the floor to sort through later. Of course, *later* I couldn't recall the meaning of my vague notes scrawled in haste or why I'd printed off numerous documents. Unsure if I'd followed a lead or not, I often repeated research. Being organized would have made more efficient use of my time and likely have saved me hundreds of research hours. I didn't start creating binders and family trees online for several years. Now I create private trees for every ancestor I trace and anyone I assist. I even create them for fictional characters in my books.

5. FOCUSED ON ONE FAMILY AT A TIME

If you hit a brick wall while researching one line, it's best to move on to another one. However, I was bopping around between ten Irish lines at the same time. If researching one line sparked an idea for a possible lead with another line, I was off to the other line. I should have kept a log and written down every thought that popped into my head rather than constantly switching directions. While researching a particular family, dozens of names swirl around in my head. It's easy for all those names to become jumbled if I'm moving around between families. Why add to the confusion?

6. DOCUMENTED SOURCES

I hear this one a lot from researchers. Despite now being more organized, I still sometimes fail to note where and when I obtained a record. An obituary usually includes the date of death and maybe the day of the week, but rarely the year. Not recording the newspaper's year on a photocopy means not recording your relative's death year. And knowing in which of the local newspapers my rural ancestors were sharing their family's life events is critical when looking for additional information.

7. CONDUCTED RESEARCH ON PLACES AND EVENTS, NOT MERELY PEOPLE

Learning about the area where your ancestors lived prior to emigrating can provide research leads. Had they come from an area known for mining or being the world's largest linen manufacturer? What historical events may have forced or prompted their decision to emigrate? Spending an afternoon reading *Scottish History for Dummies* might prove as critical to tracing your family history as months on Ancestry.com.

8. BROADENED MY RESOURCES SOONER

In the beginning I relied much too heavily on the census and online family trees, which I slowly figured out were often inaccurate. At that same time, I was searching for death records and obituaries. But I should have branched out into other historical resources much sooner, such as military documents, city directories, and naturalization papers.

9. LOOKED BEYOND IMMEDIATE FAMILY MEMBERS

Don't merely include your immediate ancestors in a family tree. Trace their siblings' spouses and children, nieces, nephews, cousins, in-laws . . . anyone you can link to the family. You never know what clues a distant relation might provide. My ancestor Eliza Turney Watson had a niece who married a man descended from the McLeans on the Isle of Mull, Scotland. My dad has dozens of McLean DNA matches and connections to this area of Scotland. This man's family quite possibly knew the Watsons or Turneys back in their homeland. I can give many examples of how tracing distant relations has proven helpful. I wished I'd started doing it much earlier in my research.

10. CREATED A GAME PLAN

Be proactive, not reactive. Granted, in the beginning I didn't know enough to be proactive and develop a plan. I flew by the seat of my knickers. But again, as a meeting planner I keep a list of all my *lists*. Yet I still find myself embarking on new research without a plan. Discovering my dad is biologically a Burke, not a Watson, has been overwhelming to say the least. I was so anxious to learn when the surname change had taken place that I was frantically analyzing DNA matches at random with no method in place. I finally said, "Whoa." I took a step back to review the information I had obtained and developed an action plan for moving forward.

44

TEN ASSUMPTIONS THAT CAN LEAD TO CREATING YOUR OWN BRICK WALLS

1. THAT YOUR PATERNAL DNA MATCHES YOUR SURNAME

My dad's paternal DNA test revealing he's biologically a Burke and not a Watson took my ancestry research in a whole new direction. I'm now on a quest to uncover family secrets and trace our newfound royal lineage. When, where, and why did our Burke surname change to Watson? Could there be a more mysterious secret for a genealogist to uncover? Now knowing what I'm looking for in DNA matches is already providing new leads.

2. THAT A PERSON WAS BURIED IN THE CEMETERY NEAREST TO HIS HOME

I mentioned having found my Coffey graves in Ireland more than ten miles away from their home. In southern Wisconsin I finally located my Flannery ancestors' graves twenty-five miles from where they'd lived. That was quite a hike in 1863. Why had they been buried so far from home? Had the cemetery had a sale on burial plots? Who knows.

3. THAT ALL THE CHILDREN IN A FAMILY SHARED THE SAME MOTHER

In an 1860 census, Henry Watson lived in Wisconsin with his wife, Bridget, and three sons. There was an eight-year gap between the youngest and the middle sons. The youngest son's birthplace was Wisconsin, and the middle son's was Ireland. Even though Bridget was born in Ireland like the rest of the family—except for the youngest son—the sons' age difference made me wonder if Henry had remarried. It turned out he'd married his second wife, Bridget, in Wisconsin. Coming across a second marriage is a huge find. The marriage record might note the couple's parents.

4. THAT A PERSON WASN'T PREVIOUSLY MARRIED

James Watson's second marriage record is the only document I've found with his parents' names. It also provided his new wife's, Anne Murdoch's, parents' surname as Cowan. I had another version of this record that didn't have parents' names, so I'd assumed Anne's maiden name was Murdoch, not Cowan. This was good to know. The 1861 Canada Census hadn't given her marital status as widowed. However, I had learned she was born in Ireland and her religious affiliation was the Church of Ireland, so she'd likely been from Northern Ireland. Families listed on the page lived in the military district in Kingston, Ontario. Anne's first husband and James had possibly served together in the military.

Meeting your spouse back then, even the second one, often wasn't a random encounter. Immigrants gravitated to areas where they had familial connections from their homeland. A spouse from a person's native country is one more clue, so having a woman's correct maiden name is critical. There's always a chance a woman may have been previously married. At the time James and Anne wed, it appears that Canadian marriage records didn't document a person's previous marital status. However, England's and Ireland's civil marriage records noted a woman as *spinster* (a dreadful term for single) or *widow*. I don't recall ever coming across that notation in Ireland's Catholic parish records. Whether or not a woman's marital status was documented depends on the time period, country, religious denomination, and other factors. Just keep in mind, if you are having difficulty locating a female ancestor's baptismal record, maybe the name you have wasn't her maiden name. Try searching for a previous marriage record.

5. THAT A DOCUMENT IS CORRECT

I've said this before, but I can't say it enough. The most reliable information is generally on documents that the person themselves provided. Death records being one of the most unreliable. If at all possible, it's critical to have a minimum of two sources with the same information before considering it accurate. This does not include an online family tree.

6. THAT A DOCUMENT'S *INCORRECT* INFORMATION ISN'T SOMEHOW VALID

I've used the three Watson siblings' death certificates as an example before because it is such a perfect one. That their correct mother, Bridget Connolly, wasn't noted on any of the documents. One certificate had the mother as Delia Grieve. I finally realized Delia was a nickname for Bridget and that the name Grieve has DNA matches with my dad. At some point a Grieve surname may come into play.

The death certificate for another sibling, Anna Barbara Watson, noted her mother's name also as Anna, not Bridget. However, I later learned that the deceased's name, Anna Barbara, was actually a combination of the woman's two grandmothers' names. Anna was her maternal grandmother, Barbara her paternal one. So even though her mother's name was incorrect, it provided great clues to both her grandmothers' identities. Anna's children had likely been told she'd been named after *grandmothers* and they remembered it as her having been named after her *mother*.

7. THAT A COUPLE WITH CHILDREN WAS MARRIED

My research in Ireland hasn't yet uncovered any out-of-wedlock births in my family lines. At a time without birth control, it's highly likely several occurred. While assisting an elderly English woman with her family research, I discovered she came from a long line of illegitimate children on both sides of her family. Most of the parents married at some point. However, when I came across a marriage record several years after a couple's children were born, I initially assumed it was for a different couple. That wasn't the case. See Tip 11, "Playing a Genealogist Sleuth, Inspector Clouseau or Sherlock Holmes?"

8. THAT A COUNTRY HAS ONLY ONE VILLAGE OR TOWN WITH A PARTICULAR NAME

In 1947 my relative James Coffey died in Balrath, Ireland, leaving a 350-acre estate worth loads of money. Wanting to visit it on an upcoming Ireland trip, I located Balrath, County Westmeath, on Google Maps. Later I returned to Google Maps to again view the town, and a Balrath in County Meath appeared. It turned out there are *nine* Balrath towns in Counties Meath and Westmeath. I was able to determine which Balrath was the one I was looking for, and we visited the estate. I discuss my journey to locate this home in Tip 49, "Walking in Your Ancestors' Footsteps: Finding Their Family Homesteads."

9. THAT YOU KNOW *HOW* YOU ARE RELATED TO A FAMILY LINE

Ancestry.com recently "tweaked" members' DNA ethnicities, supposedly to improve the accuracy of the estimates. My dad's Scottish and Irish decreased, and his Norwegian increased from 45 percent to 58 percent. His mother was supposedly 100 percent Norwegian. His father had no known Norwegian. So where is his other 8 percent coming from? It's likely coming from his Scottish or Irish ancestors. With the early Norman invasions in both Ireland and Scotland, I have found the Normans came from sturdy stock and their DNA often lingers for twenty-plus generations. Yet I should no longer assume a Norwegian match is from my dad's maternal side.

I've been trying to determine the connection of the Watson family from southern Wisconsin that moved to Chicago and worked for my Watson's steam-fitting company. The fact that the two families only had a few children's names in common made me wonder how close of a connection they shared. I'm now finding my dad has numerous MacDonald DNA matches. The mother of this other Watson family was Catherine MacDonald from Scotland—homeland of our Watsons. Perhaps these Watsons were related through the MacDonald line. Families often traveled in the same circle. Much of rural Ireland didn't marry outside their townland, so cousins knowingly or unknowingly often wed. My dad has hundreds of distant DNA matches in County Galway with almost no common surnames. It's hard to know where to begin. When you are analyzing DNA matches back five-plus generations, don't assume because the surname is a match that is where the connection lies.

10. MAKING ASSUMPTIONS EVEN BASED ON FACTS

I hit a brick wall with my Watsons when James's wife died and the following year's 1861 census noted he was living with a Catherine whose status was married. I assumed it was James's new wife. In my defense, that wasn't a wild assumption. However, she was twenty-five years younger. Even though at that time women frequently married older men, that was a big age difference. James Jr. wasn't living at home, so I wondered if he was off somewhere and his new wife had remained behind.

I had a genealogist search for either of the James's marriage to a Catherine. No record was located. However, he found an 1861 marriage record for James Sr. and an Anne Murdoch. What was the chance that James had remarried *twice* within a year after his wife's death? And James Jr. married an Eliza a few years later. No death certificate was found for a Catherine Watson. It is likely that Catherine, the wife of a Watson relative, had gone to live with James after his wife's death to help care for his two teenage daughters. This demonstrates the importance of following your instincts and conducting further research rather than accepting what would seem to be true.

45

A GENEALOGY SUPPORT
NETWORK:

JUST WHAT THE DOCTOR ORDERED

Genealogical research can be lonely, sitting at my computer for long hours by myself—or with my assistant, Frankie, my tuxedo cat. Especially during the wee hours of the morning when the house is quiet except for my fingers tapping against the keyboard and an occasional ancestor talking in my head. Yet family historians and genealogists in Ireland and the UK are already up sipping tea, perusing the internet. What a perfect time for me to reach out to the living, not merely the dead.

I am working at increasing my genealogy network through online social media groups and forums. After all, this is my tribe. They understand my frustration when I need an Irish baptismal record for December 31, 1823, and that parish's register begins January 1, 1824. They join in my celebration when I discover my ancestor's actual signature on his naturalization papers. They laugh when all I want for Christmas is a peek at the destroyed 1890 US Census. They understand my obsession, er, passion for genealogy, unlike many friends and family members.

One of my favorite Facebook groups is The Genealogy Squad. The group administrators include Cyndi Ingle (Cyndi's List), Drew

Smith (Genealogy Guys), and Cari Taplin (Genealogy Pants). It's the perfect place for asking questions and discussing research challenges. If you aren't familiar with Cyndi's List, www.cyndislist.com, I highly recommend it. I've used the website for years.

Deidre Erin Denton offers great tidbits of advice on her Facebook page Twisted Twigs on Gnarled Branches Genealogy. If I'm having a bad day, her page will perk me up with a humorous graphic about cemeteries, research, or family dynamics. One of my other preferred pages is Genealogy Tip of the Day, which also has a website, www.genealogytipoftheday.com. If this is the first you've heard of Michael John Neill's site, you've missed years of tips, but no worries. He recently compiled hundreds of past tips into a book *Genealogy Tip of the Day*. You can catch up on several years of tips in a few days or read a tip daily.

Besides providing emotional support, fellow researchers can offer suggestions and possibly help you break down a brick wall. I belong to a group whose members are skilled at deciphering hard-to-read documents. When I couldn't decide if the mother's name on a Watson death certificate was Delia *Turney*—grossly misspelled—or possibly *Gweres*, I asked for opinions. The general consensus was that the name was Grieve, a Scottish surname. Sure enough, my dad has several DNA matches with Grieves. That might be it. However, the name also looks a bit like Guire.

As I've mentioned, my knowledge about DNA research is limited. Besides purchasing a reference book on analyzing DNA test results, I have joined numerous Facebook groups associated with GEDmatch's DNA surname and location projects. Tagging DNA matches in a post is a great way to start a discussion group. Many of these researchers belong to other groups and can recommend ones you might find beneficial.

46

A GAME OF TRUE OR FALSE:

GENEALOGY FACT OR MYTH?

The following are statements I've heard many times over the years and which I believed to be true. However, my genealogical research has disproved several of them. As I've said numerous times, never make assumptions when conducting research. However, the problem with assuming is you often don't realize that's what you're doing when you believe it to be true.

MOST HISTORICAL RECORDS WERE DESTROYED IN A FIRE. FALSE

Replacing the word *most* with *many* would make it a true statement. It often seems like most records I need didn't survive. More times than not, when I've found a priest willing to assist me with obtaining a marriage or baptismal record, it turns out it went up in flames along with the church the day *after* the needed date. A fire having destroyed the 1890 US Census poses a challenge for researchers. However, that's a minor challenge when you compare it to Ireland having lost all pre-1901 censuses in a fire.

THERE WERE MANY OUT-OF-WEDLOCK BIRTHS. TRUE

This shouldn't be a surprise when there was no birth control, yet I was shocked at the number of illegitimate children noted in some church registers. I learned early on that Irish Catholic couples ensured their marriage was on file so all births were seen as legitimate. Yet my Tip 11 demonstrates the great length an English couple went to in having their born-out-of-wedlock children baptized. FYI, Scotland historical records referred to this as a *natural* birth. I haven't come across any *documented* natural births in my family's history. However, DNA matches have proven there were several.

THE IRISH ALL DROPPED THE O' FROM THEIR LAST NAMES WHEN IMMIGRATING. FALSE

When I started researching Irish documents, I expected to find O'Coffey, O'Flannery, O'Daly . . . but not one O' prefixed a family name. Many people dropped the Irish-sounding O' or Mc/Mac from the beginning of their names back in the seventeenth and eighteenth centuries to prevent further discrimination while under English rule. However, the belief that the Irish, and other ethnicities, usually Americanized their names when immigrating is overstated.

THE MAYFLOWER BROUGHT THE FIRST SETTLERS TO AMERICA. FALSE

Mayflower passengers were not actually the *first* settlers. The Jamestown, Virginia, colony was thirteen years old before the Mayflower's arrival. And historians estimate that by 1610, Britain and other European countries had several hundred fishing vessels operating out of New England and Newfoundland. So there were some settlers in America pre-Mayflower. However, I question the accuracy of the large number of my DNA matches who claim their ancestors settled in America years before the Mayflower. And that 35 million people worldwide claim to be descended from Mayflower passengers when only five women survived that first winter to go on to bear children.

I once read how a man debunked his family history recorded in the family's Bible, claiming they were descended from Mayflower passengers. The man's research had proven his ancestors had shared a common surname with a couple on board the ship, but they weren't that same couple. Not only was this poor guy stripped of his Mayflower descendant badge but fifteen generations of relatives. Never assume a tree in your family Bible doesn't contain errors because it was handwritten by an ancestor generations ago.

MANY EMIGRANTS CAME OVER AS STOWAWAYS. FALSE

I mentioned previously that a ship manifest debunked my family folklore about our ancestor having come to America as a stowaway on a potato boat. I recently read that this is a common myth passed down in family folklore. Maybe my passion for writing fiction came from a long line of storytellers who preferred an adventurous, romanticized tale of our ancestor emigrating rather than the harsh reality that he'd fled Ireland to escape a famine and other hardships.

HALF THE WOMEN DIED IN CHILDBIRTH. FALSE

Statements like this one always made me wonder why women had kids if they knew it was going to kill them. I wouldn't have. I was expecting to find that most of my female ancestors had died during child-bearing years. I've confirmed one woman's death resulted from childbirth, but many of my female ancestors outlived their children.

OUR FOREBEARS DIED YOUNG. FALSE

An estimated one in five Civil War–era children died before age five from illnesses that are now preventable. Yet in 1850, if a person had reached age 40, he was likely to live to almost seventy years old. While perusing old newspapers, I've seen numerous articles celebrating the hundredth birthday of a local centenarian. I question the accuracy of these milestone birthdays when many people didn't know their birth years or didn't have the math skills to calculate their ages based on birth years. Whether ninety or a hundred years old, I'm sure the celebration of life was well deserved and a great time was had by all.

PEOPLE DIDN'T DIVORCE BACK THEN. FALSE

It might not have been as easy back then, but I have obtained US divorce papers from the late 1800s. In Ireland divorce was illegal until 1997, and it's still not easy to obtain one. Maybe a few of my ancestors left Ireland to escape a bad marriage rather than a famine or ethnic persecution.

WOMEN NOWADAYS HAVE CHILDREN MUCH LATER IN LIFE. FALSE

Women might *start* families later in life than previous generations, delaying having children until their late thirties and forties, when earlier generations began families in their twenties. But in the 1800s, a woman often had ten kids by the age of forty and continued giving birth into her early fifties. Having children at an older age is not a new trend.

47

RESEARCHING YOUR
IRISH ANCESTORS

Ireland can pose a bit of a challenge for genealogists. A large percentage of the country's historical records were destroyed in 1922 during the Irish Civil War when an explosion caused a fire at Dublin's Public Record Office of Ireland. The documents lost include pre-1901 censuses—except for a few fragments—and over a thousand Church of Ireland (Protestant) parish registers for baptisms, marriages, and burials. Quite disheartening, yet don't give up before you start. The fact that I've successfully researched more than a dozen of my Irish lines in the 1800s demonstrates that it is possible with a bit of perseverance. Research prior to 1800 becomes more difficult.

On a positive note, there is a project underway to retrieve copies of all available lost documents housed in Ireland's and other countries' archives that is scheduled for completion in 2022. This undertaking is headed by Trinity College Dublin, in collaboration with the National Archives, the UK's National Archives, the Public Record Office of Northern Ireland, and the Irish Manuscripts Commission.

The most critical surviving records include the following:

- The 1901 and 1911 Irish censuses
- Civil (government) registration records, which began in 1864
- Nearly 50 percent of the Church of Ireland parish registers (Thankfully, many clergymen hadn't submitted their registers to Dublin as mandated.)
- Baptismal, marriage, and burial records for Roman Catholics, Presbyterians, and Methodists, which were not housed at the Public Record Office
- Griffith's Valuation—the primary source of land and property records compiled from 1847 to 1864
- Indexes to wills and probate bonds

The main sites I use for Ireland research are Findmypast, Roots Ireland, Ancestry.com, and FamilySearch. Findmypast has the largest online Irish family history collection, with over 140 million records. Ancestry.com has approximately 40 million records. Although Roots Ireland only has about 22 million records, it boasts the most extensive searchable database of Catholic parish records. I find it one of the easiest sites to search, especially by county. Each county provides a contact email for their genealogical society if you have a question. You sometimes have to be creative when searching for misspelled surnames. Also check out the site's blog for up-to-date news.

Before you begin researching your ancestor in Ireland, try to determine an approximate birth year and from which county he hailed. Notice I said *approximate* year because few Irish knew their birth year. My Irish ancestors' birth years documented on US or Canada records have rarely matched the baptismal records in Ireland. Knowing the county your ancestor lived in is important, especially if he had a common name. I have learned most of my ancestors' home counties from obituaries, gravestones, and naturalization records. Death certificates rarely list more than the country of birth.

What if you have exhausted every resource in your ancestor's country of emigration and still can't determine his birth county?

Genealogist John Grenham's website, www.johngrenham.com, is a great place to start.

GENEALOGIST JOHN GRENHAM'S WEBSITE

In addition to his website, John Grenham has written numerous genealogical and historical books on Ireland. Thankfully, and surprisingly, I discovered his website early on in my research. The site allows limited free access, then requires a nominal fee.

If you haven't a clue where your ancestor lived in Ireland, you can search his surname on this site. A map will plot the surname based on the households included in the 1847–1864 Griffith's Valuation—land and property records. My Flannery surname map has clusters of households concentrated in five western counties, including Mayo, where my ancestors lived. The surname is absent from the Ulster region and rare in the other counties. Right off I'd narrowed down the likelihood that my Flannerys were from one of the top five counties.

An interesting point—in the middle of these clusters is the largest concentration of Flannerys living in Clonmacnoise, County Offaly. This monastic site had close associations with the kings of Connacht (the northwestern province of Ireland, including County Mayo). At one time the Flannery clan was likely dominant in that region and then slowly dispersed to the surrounding areas. The website also maps out surnames based on numerous other resources, such as Roman Catholic births and the 1901 and 1911 censuses.

Additionally, you can determine the most common areas for your ancestor's forename. If it wasn't Patrick, John, Mary, or another popular name, you're in luck! Festus, a unique first name in Ireland, can be narrowed down to the Clifden area in West Galway. When I was researching my Barbara Watson, I discovered that 75 percent of the Barbaras born from 1864 to 1913 were in County Galway.

If your ancestor's obituary merely states he was from Killybegs, no county noted, you can search place names. You'll discover there were two Killybegs in Wexford, one in Donegal, and one in Kildare. Never Google a place name in Ireland, and go with the first one that pops up. Many townland and village names were repeated.

The site has a nifty tool that allows you to input any known details about your ancestor to receive an automated "Personal Ancestor Report." The results include everything from family histories to historical record categories containing your ancestor's name. I discovered a Coffey two-volume genealogy book published in Denmark and housed at the National Library of Ireland. Check out John Grenham's site and see what other resources it has to offer.

RELIGIOUS AFFILIATION AND CHURCH RECORDS

If your ancestors immigrated to Canada, the country's census noted people's religion. Unfortunately, the US Census didn't record religious affiliation. Knowing your ancestor's religion can help narrow down where he lived in Ireland. In the mid-1800s, about 75 percent of the Republic of Ireland was Roman Catholic and 25 percent belonged to the Church of Ireland or the Presbyterian church. The Church of Ireland (the Anglican/Protestant church) was the official state church from 1690 to 1870, subject to parliamentary control. The largest percentage of Protestants lived in the Ulster region, where counties were as much as 80 percent Protestant. That's not to say some Protestants didn't live in other areas, but a much smaller percentage. Western Ireland was predominantly Roman Catholic. There are numerous online maps identifying Ireland's religious breakdown by areas.

Roots Ireland, www.rootsireland.ie, includes approximately 90 percent of Roman Catholic records and 60 percent of the available Church of Ireland records. The site is continually adding more baptismal, marriage, and burial records. Burial records are a rare find in the Roman Catholic Church and much more common for the Church of Ireland. The records that exist vary greatly by county and parish. Each county on Roots Ireland will list the available records and their timeframe. I've found baptismal and marriage records for parishes in Counties Westmeath and Wicklow back to the late 1700s. Whereas in Castlebar, County Mayo, the first baptismal records in my ancestors' parish date from 1838.

Findmypast offers a large percentage of Ireland's church records, and Ancestry.com and FamilySearch have select records. The National Library of Ireland has digitized 98 percent of the Catholic parish registers for Ireland and Northern Ireland. It is a free website. However, the records are not currently indexed or searchable by name. You will need to know the county of birth and also the parish, since each county has dozens of parishes. Otherwise you'll spend weeks reading through the original registers until you possibly come across the needed record. The site is located at www.nli.ie/en/parish-register.aspx.

Remember to document all witnesses and sponsors noted on parish records. If you're unsure why that's important, see Tip 24, "He's No Joe Blow: The Importance of Sponsors and Witnesses."

CIVIL RECORDS

In 1845 Ireland's government began requiring civil records for non-Catholic marriages only, before the mandate extended to births, deaths, and marriages for people of all religions in 1864. A unified system of civil registration then operated until the partition of Ireland in 1921. After that time, Northern Ireland and the Republic of Ireland kept their own records with different formats and information. Death records contain the date, location, and marital status (no spouse's name). This document's most helpful detail is usually the informant's name, most often a spouse, child, or other relation.

You can view the civil records indexes and a large number of original images for free at www.irishgenealogy.ie. The index can also be viewed on major research sites.

1901 AND 1911 CENSUSES

Ireland's 1901 and 1911 censuses are the only complete surviving censuses available to the public. The 1921 census was delayed until 1926 because of the Irish War of Independence. It will be released in January 2027 due to a 100-year privacy policy. Fragments exist for a few counties for the 1821 to 1851 censuses. The 1841 and 1851 censuses list members of the household not living at home on census night and also family members who'd died since 1831 or 1841. But I won't dwell on what information we *don't* have and that my ancestors all emigrated prior to the 1901 census. I have used both censuses to trace forward family members who remained in Ireland. And searching your ancestor's townland may turn up unknown relations. You can access the census records for free at the National Archives of Ireland, www.census.nationalarchives.ie.

On the evening of the census, the head of household completed and signed a number of original returns. The enumerator completed three statistical returns pertaining to religious denominations, classification of buildings, and out-offices and farmsteads. The 1901 and 1911 censuses include the following information for each family member: name, age, sex, relationship to head of the household, religion, occupation, marital status, county or country of birth. The census also notes an individual's ability to read, write, and speak the Irish language and whether the person was deaf, dumb, blind, an idiot, imbecile, or lunatic. Thankfully, the times have changed for socially acceptable terms and how handicaps are now viewed. In addition, the 1911 census documented how many years a couple had been married and their number of children both living and deceased. This is helpful when using the traditional family naming pattern as a guideline for locating unknown children.

STANDARD CENSUS SUBSTITUTES

I have utilized the following documents regarded as standard census substitutes for the late 1700s and 1800s. Unfortunately, these records only provide the heads of households' names.

Griffith's Valuation. This is the most valuable document substitute for the census, detailing land and property records. It is a great resource for narrowing down your ancestor's location in Ireland if unknown. The information was compiled from 1847 to 1864 in a series of 301 volumes for the purpose of taxing tenants based on the yearly income the property could be expected to produce. That figure was used to calculate the local taxation. Tenants with a holding valued at less than £5 annually were exempt, but their landlord was liable for the tax. Sadly, this caused many landlords to evict smaller tenants and contributed to the wave of evictions during the famine and second half of the nineteenth century.

See Tip 18 for further details on the Griffith's Valuation. The document can be found at Ask About Ireland, www.askaboutireland.ie/griffith-valuation.

The Tithe Applotment Books. These books were compiled between 1823 and 1837 to determine the tax amount occupiers of agricultural holdings over one acre owed the Church of Ireland—the state church. There is a book for almost every civil parish. An entry notes the tenant's name, the amount of leased land, and the tax owed. Because the tithes were levied on agricultural land, urban areas were not included. You can search the books at www.titheapplotmentbooks.nationalarchives.ie.

Flax Report. The Irish Linen Board's 1796 Flax Growers List included 60,000 individuals, noting the person's name, parish, and county. The purpose of the report was to award farmers spinning wheels based on the number of acres planted. Donegal and Tyrone received the highest number of wheels. Counties Dublin and Wicklow were not included in the list. Either they received no wheels, or the records have been lost.

See Tip 29 for further details on the report, which can be viewed at www.failteromhat.com.

CREATIVE CENSUS SUBSTITUTES

The following are merely a few of the creative resources available on Ancestry.com, FamilySearch, or Findmypast. For additional resources, see the sites' updated card catalogs. Before you search a database, verify if the whole of Ireland is included or merely select counties. Some records only survive from certain counties.

Dog License Registrations, 1810–1926. I learned that my relative James Coffey owned two red collies from 1912 to 1916. This dog was bred for herding sheep. I found this interesting since I'm quite fond of sheep. Not only does this register help you track your ancestor prior to the 1901 census and after the 1911 one, it provides a bit of insight into the person.

Ireland, Petty Session Court Registers, 1818–1919. From 1872 to 1883, my relation John Coffey was the defendant in four petty court sessions. Curiously, his brother Andrew and his father, James, lived in the same town but had no records. These registers provide some fascinating reading for your family biography. In one case, John owed a Patrick Lynch a day's wage. Interestingly, John's grandmother was Bridget *Lynch*, so Patrick was likely a relation. Witnesses can also provide leads for other possible relatives.

The register can help narrow down when a person died, moved, or emigrated. In 1883, shortly before immigrating to the US, John had a last hurrah that landed him in jail for drunkenness for eight days, costing him two schillings. John also had two drunkenness charges that occurred in Mullingar. Today, Mullingar is a half-hour drive from where he'd lived. That would have been quite the jaunt in the 1880s. However, Mullingar would have been a major market center at the time, so John might have celebrated a successful sales day with a few too many pints.

Irish Reproductive Loan Funds (Known on Ancestry.com

as the **Ireland, Sustainability Loan Fund, 1812–1868**). These short-term loans required guarantors, usually close family members or neighbors. The purpose of the loan was for people to purchase items such as farming tools, livestock, or building materials for a barn and outbuildings that would "reproduce" the loan's value, ensuring repayment. Most records date from 1824 to 1846 and are a critical resource for information on people who died during the Great Famine or who emigrated during that time. Records survive for the following counties: Cork, Clare, Galway, Kerry, Leitrim, Limerick, Mayo, Roscommon, Sligo, and Tipperary.

I found many records for my Flannerys in County Mayo. When a Thomas Rielley borrowed money from the bank, *three* of my Flannery relatives were the guarantors. Thomas must have been a relative or great friend for the men to have assumed the financial responsibility if he defaulted on the loan. The three men were once again guarantors for a widow, Bridget Flannery, who was likely a sister-in-law or aunt.

Ireland's National School List. These registers include former schools from twenty-four counties. Information in the records varies but will usually contain the child's name, birth year, home address and previous address, religion, and occupation of parents—but unfortunately not their names. You can view the list for a fee at Findmypast.

Muster/Militia Rolls. I am using muster rolls for 1805 to 1825 to locate a possible ancestor in the Donegal Regiment. These roll calls of officers and men in military regiments from the seventeenth to the twentieth centuries are housed at the National Library of Ireland, located in Dublin, www.nli.ie. In theory, every able-bodied man was required to serve. The militia muster rolls list the principal landowners and the men available for military service. Since these records are usually quite extensive, it is more economical to hire a local genealogist to retrieve the documents than to request them directly through the library.

Other Census Resources. The previously mentioned John

Grenham's website and Roots Ireland offer lists of census substitutes for each county in Ireland.

ADDITIONAL IRELAND RESEARCH SOURCES

The Public Record Office of Northern Ireland offers incredible online research guides. Even if your ancestors weren't from Northern Ireland, you will find many helpful hints: www.nidirect.gov.uk/articles/your-family-tree-series

Irish Genealogy Toolkit: www.irish-genealogy-toolkit.com

Military Archives: www.militaryarchives.ie/en/home

The Irish Genealogical Research Society: www.irishancestors.ie

Ireland Reaching Out: www.irelandxo.com

TRACING YOUR FAMILY
BACKWARD AND THEN FORWARD
TO FIND LIVING RELATIVES

I'm surprised at the number of family historians who spend years tracing their family trees back generations to their ancestors' homelands and then quit. When I reach that point, I celebrate with a glass of wine and begin tracing my ancestors' family members forward in hopes of one day sharing a pint with living relatives in Ireland. Over the past ten years, I've met numerous Irish relations from three of my family lines and have enjoyed many pints. I've learned family history —including a few family secrets—that I would never have uncovered on Ancestry.com. I have exchanged priceless family photos. And best of all, I've visited our ancestors' childhood homes, which I recount in Tip 49, "Walking in Your Ancestors' Footsteps: Finding Their Family Homesteads." I've used several methods to locate relatives, including connecting with an owner of an Ancestry.com family tree, traditional genealogy methods, and online supersleuthing.

At the beginning of this book, I mentioned tracing my Daly line forward thanks to unrelated genealogist Jane Daly locating a 1960 newspaper article about Michael Daly's daughter (my Patrick's niece) having been struck and killed by a truck. With help from the internet, I found a descendant who belonged to a local Lions Club, and a board member put me in touch with my first living relative in Ireland.

Next, I traced another one of Michael's daughters forward. Using the Irish Newspaper Archives, www.irishnewsarchive.com, I pieced together birth, marriage, and death records for a daughter who married and had three children. I discovered that her one daughter married a reverend, and I was able to locate his church. Unfortunately, it turned out he'd passed away a year prior, in 2008, but my relation, Joyce, was still living in that same area. Thanks to an article on the church's website, I found the first picture of a living Irish relative. I sent Joyce a letter and received a lovely response. She put me in touch with her niece Charlotte, who had done a bit of research on the Dalys, including locating the family home in County Westmeath. Two years later on a trip to Ireland, I met Joyce and her two children, William and Patricia, along with Charlotte and Peter.

Back in 2008 I began piecing together my Flannery family tree. It was a bit challenging since the earliest surviving Roman Catholic records for my ancestors' parish in County Mayo dated from 1838. As luck would have it, the family members that emigrated were born prior to that year. This made it critical that I obtain every bit of information I could here in the US. That included marriage and birth records from Baltimore, where the family first lived before settling in Wisconsin. Luckily, the parents and five adult sons' families moved to the same area in southern Wisconsin. However, one son remained in Baltimore. A descendant of his and I have shared research and kept in touch.

Once I compiled as much information as I could, I began comparing my tree with others on Ancestry.com. After a bit of searching, I found someone in the US related to my Flannerys back six generations. I reached out to him and discovered that he'd recently visited our Flannerys' homeland, where he'd met a relative, Patrick Flannery. He was kind enough to put me in touch with Patrick, who would turn out to be the first Irish relative I'd meet.

Out of Patrick *Coffey's* seven known siblings, I successfully traced five of them forward. Three had immigrated to America, while two had remained in County Westmeath, Ireland. Luckily, his brother Andrew stayed in their hometown, where he had several children who lived to adulthood. Three of them remained in Ireland, but only one married and had children. Thankfully, this daughter, Catherine, was born and married in Andrew's home parish. In the 1901 and 1911 censuses, Catherine's family lived in County Offaly. After locating a 1930s marriage record for her daughter, I was off and running. Her married surname was an uncommon one, making the family easier to trace. Her obituary noted the names of two living sons. Bingo!

Using Ireland's online phonebook and "people search" sites, I obtained the addresses of several potential candidates with the sons' names. I mailed letters to a half dozen possibilities and waited anxiously for a response. Thankfully, a letter made it into one of the son's mailboxes. Although he wasn't interested in genealogy, he kindly forwarded my letter to his brother, Bernard, who was interested. Bernard had limited information on his grandma Catherine, so I shared my research, and he shared some lovely photos, including one of his grandma's family circa 1900. I've enjoyed high tea at a fancy Dublin hotel with Bernard and his wife, Nuala. My husband and I recently celebrated Christmas with their entire family. But my most memorable moment with Bernard was when we visited our Coffey ancestors' homesteads.

Turn the page to read about my adventures visiting my ancestors' childhood homes with my newfound Irish rellies Patrick, Bernard, and Charlotte!

Bernard's grandma Catherine Coffey's family in Ireland,
circa 1900

49

WALKING IN YOUR
ANCESTORS' FOOTSTEPS:

FINDING THEIR FAMILY HOMESTEADS

I have located several ancestors' family homesteads thanks to newfound relations living in Ireland, stalking a mailman, a Griffith's Valuation land map, and a wee bit of Irish luck. In 2010 my mother, cousin, and I visited our Flannery and Daly homesteads. I'll never forget those moments when I first stepped on Flannery land and when I walked, or rather crawled, through the glassless window frame into my ancestor Patrick Daly's childhood home.

Patrick Flannery was the first Irish relative I met. He still lives on the Flannery land in County Mayo. The foundation of our ancestors' house sits on the edge of his property down the hill from his newer home. He took us on a tour of the surrounding land once occupied by mostly Flannery families and shared stories about our ancestors' lives in the 1800s. We snapped photos of relatives' former homes as well as their permanent ones when Patrick introduced us to family members at the local cemetery. We enjoyed a wonderful homemade meal with authentic Irish brown bread, old family photos, and stories with Patrick, his wife, Geraldine, and daughter, Alison. It was one of the most memorable days of my life. I didn't sleep a wink that night, still on a genealogy high.

Later that trip, we met our Daly cousin Charlotte and her husband, Peter. My mom's great-grandfather, Patrick, immigrated to America, while his brother Michael, Charlotte's great-grandfather, remained in Ireland. A few years earlier, Charlotte and Peter had located the Daly home in County Westmeath. We visited the deserted stone cottage surrounded by green rolling fields our family had farmed 150 years ago. Thick vines meandered up the home's rough exterior, and a horseshoe embedded between two stones had brought luck to both the surviving dwelling and us. The cottage's weathered wooden door was blocked closed from the inside, so we crawled through the glassless window frame into the home.

Standing on the dirt floor surrounded by chipped white-washed walls now green with moss, I envisioned Patrick's mother cooking stew or potatoes in a large cast-iron pot in the massive fireplace that consumed an entire wall. And above me, a metal roof now covered the original thatched one. Ivy and straw dangled from pegged wooden beams, which the two young boys might have carved their names into when they should have been sleeping in the loft. Now gone, the upper structure would have benefited from the fireplace's rising heat during the damp, cold winters. Charlotte and Peter described details about how the family's life would have been in the two-room dwelling. They also shared a neighbor's story, who'd recalled as a child his parents threatening to drop him off at Agnes Daly's if he misbehaved. That gave us all a laugh. Michael's daughter's reputation might have been why the woman had never married and lived in her childhood home without electricity or indoor plumbing until her death in 1979. At that time, it wouldn't have been uncommon for folks in rural Ireland, especially the elderly, to have retained their ancestors' way of life.

As I stood there gazing around at the dwelling's dirt floors and moldy walls, the scent of wet earth mingling with fresh rain in the air, a peaceful feeling came over me. I felt at home. I've traveled the world for both business and pleasure, but until that day, I'd never felt such an overwhelming sense of belonging in another country. When I walked out the rusted gate as my ancestor Patrick had over a hundred years ago, unlike him, I knew I would one day return. Since then, I've taken numerous family members to visit the Daly homestead. Three years after this trip, my husband and I bought an 1887 schoolhouse in my Coffeys' homeland. Unlike the Daly home, it's renovated, without mold or dirt floors. I'm not made of the same sturdy stock as Agnes Daly.

Prior to our next Ireland trip two years later, I connected with Bernard, a Coffey relation living in Ireland. His great-grandfather Andrew Coffey—my ancestor Patrick's brother—was the only known family member who remained in Ireland. Bernard hadn't known his grandmother Catherine's birth location. Thanks to the Griffith's Valuation, I found the family home and was able to pinpoint the house's approximate location on the record's map. If Google Maps offered the ability to drive virtually down a road at that time, I wasn't familiar with it. An Irish friend living nearby took a photo of the home for me. Later visiting the home where Bernard and my ancestors Patrick and Andrew had grown up was a bit emotional for Bernard and Nuala, my mom, and me.

The home's current owners welcomed us with a four-course meal and were quite interested to learn about our family who'd occupied the house for the hundred years before their family, starting in the early 1900s. The house was much larger than the Dalys' cottage, but both families had merely rented the properties from English landlords for generations. Andrew's son James would later inherit a 350-acre estate from a maternal uncle, valued at nearly a million euros in today's dollars. Too bad brothers Patrick and Andrew hadn't lived to see the day a Coffey *owned* rather than *leased* the land they'd farmed in Ireland.

I discovered that James Coffey had inherited this valuable estate when genealogist Jane Daly came across a 1947 ad in both Irish and Australian newspapers searching for James's half brother, heir to the estate. When I mentioned this find to Bernard, he vaguely recalled visiting the estate as a young boy, an impressive house with steps leading up to the entrance. James's half brother was never located, so the estate had gone into probate, eventually inherited by Bernard's mother and other relations. Anxious to see the place, we drove around the area where it was located. After an hour of cruising down every narrow country road, we found ourselves following a mailman. Who better to know the local homes than a mailman? When Bernard described the home, the man suggested two possibilities, including the Balrath House. What an impressive sounding name. Yet the estate was 350 acres, so I shouldn't have been surprised.

The mailman's directions led us to a large plaque in a gated stone fence that read Balrath House. We drove slowly through the open gate and down a long driveway that disappeared into a cluster of massive oak trees. We gasped at the sight of a deserted stately home with steps leading up to the entrance, just as Bernard had described. Also, numerous outbuildings and a new metal structure housed what appeared to be a feed mill. A man, who turned out to be the owner, approached our car. When we explained our relative had likely lived there, he told us the previous owners on the land records included a James Coffey. Not having offered up our relative's name, Bernard and I teared up. If the owner hadn't been there working that day, he said the locked gate would have prevented us from discovering the home. He wasn't aware that I've been known to climb through windows and over a few fences while conducting genealogical research in Ireland.

I highly recommend locating your ancestor's birth home. It will be an emotional journey that cannot be matched. If you are unable to visit it in person, have someone take a photo of it, or better yet a video. Nothing brings an ancestor's past to life like seeing his child-hood home. The road he walked down and the trees he climbed. The fields he and his father plowed. Or the fireplace where she helped her mother prepare family meals and sat in front of it spinning wool while singing a song to keep time with the rhythm of her task. Next on my list is locating my Butlers' home in County Wicklow. Maybe I'll discover the home thanks to another kind mailman or an elderly man walking a dog down a narrow country road. However it happens, it's sure to be another adventure.

Patrick Coffey's childhood home in
County Westmeath, Ireland

Patrick Daly's childhood home in
Kilbeggan, County Westmeath, Ireland

Touring Flannery land with Patrick Flannery in County Mayo, Ireland

50

I'VE DONE EVERYTHING POSSIBLE BUT STILL CAN'T TRACE MY FAMILY LINE . . .

HAVE YOU CLIMBED MOUNT EVEREST?

Originally, I'd included the following statement in my tip about how your assumptions can build brick walls: *I've done everything possible but still can't trace my ancestors.* Then I wondered if that statement is actually an *assumption*, or does it stem from a person's frustration, inexperience, or other source? Some people say it with such conviction that I find myself momentarily believing that they've obtained thousands of documents from online sources and every church, archive, and possible known relation. I think many people expect family research to be much easier than it is. After all, that Ancestry.com commercial illustrated how you merely click a green leaf—the Hint icon—to reveal the mystery behind your ancestors. Knowing how hard I work at genealogical research, my husband always joked, "Hey, have you tried clicking that leaf?" Not funny.

As an event planner, I've had the opportunity to see numerous keynote speakers. The most memorable and inspirational one talked about her climb up Mount Everest. I wasn't even going to attend the session because I can't comprehend anyone's desire to climb a mountain. I hate cold weather, snow, and outdoor winter sports. Yet minutes into her talk I realized how strongly I could relate to her message. She compared the challenge of climbing a mountain to achieving other goals in life. Her talk turned out to be a pivotal point in my writing journey. After ten years of rejections and no publishing contract, my muse was on hiatus and I considered giving up writing. While listening to the speaker, I found myself thinking, *I can't give up. I'm three-quarters of the way up the mountain. I have to keep climbing.* The same is true with genealogical research.

She explained that when climbing Mount Everest, it takes ten days to reach Base Camp at 17,500 feet. The average time from Base Camp to the summit, another 12,000 feet up, is forty days. Why does it take so much longer to go a shorter distance? Your body has to acclimate to the higher altitude and lower oxygen levels. From Base Camp you climb to Camp One, spend the night, then return to Base Camp. The next day you're back to Camp One, spend a night, then up to Camp Two, spend a night, and back to Base Camp. The entire climb is a series of ups and downs before finally reaching the summit.

The point is, a setback is often necessary to enable you to achieve your goal. When conducting ancestry research, you may have to head down many wrong paths before you head down the right one. After months of researching an ancestor and scouring resources for a handful of documents, you might determine the person is not actually your ancestor. You'd headed down the wrong path. Not only can this be an emotional setback but also a financial one, making it even more devastating. Yet you shouldn't consider ruling out a possible ancestor as a setback but rather as the opportunity to head down the correct path. You might be a bit gun-shy and disheartened, so take a necessary breather before embarking on your next climb. During the past seven years while researching the Watsons, I've been up and down the mountain so many times I've lost count. On a few occasions, I even made it mere feet from the summit. Currently, I'm back at Camp One.

GENEALOGY BASE CAMP

Something has sparked your curiosity to trace your ancestry. Maybe you saw a family research commercial or a friend just discovered that her ancestor was English nobility. My grandpa Watson's father abandoned him when he was two years old. We had no knowledge of our family history. Watson sounded English, so we'd always assumed the family had emigrated from England. One day I had a burning desire to know the truth.

Base Camp is the stage where you become familiar with the industry giants such as FamilySearch or Ancestry.com and slowly learn to navigate the sites and what they offer. You might find yourself so enthralled with the census that you never discover other available indexes in the card catalog. You also gather as much information as you can from family members, including birth and death dates, in hopes of locating an obituary or a birth certificate. Everything is exciting while you prepare for this new adventure. You are packing your gear and making a plan. Just like climbing Mount Everest, Genealogy Base Camp is merely the beginning of your journey.

BASE CAMP TO CAMP ONE

Now the real climb begins. You create a family tree using software or online at Ancestry.com, Wiki, or another site. Your tree has few limbs and hasn't taken root. Your limited resources aren't turning up any new information, so it's time to expand your horizon. Check out genealogy blogs and read a how-to research book for some additional ideas and direction, such as reviewing city directories and locating naturalization papers and other critical documents.

What little Watson information I had was obtained from my grandpa's parents' marriage certificate. It noted James Watson was a steamfitter in Chicago and his parents were James Watson III (the suffix is my addition) and Bertha Conners. According to the baptismal certificate I'd found for a James Watson born in Chicago circa our James's birth date, his mother was Bertha *Youngren*. James had her first name correct, but how hadn't he known his mother's maiden name? My dad was skeptical that I'd found *our* James's record. So I trekked back down the mountain to Base Camp to search for more marriage and baptismal records.

BASE CAMP TO CAMP ONE TO CAMP TWO . . . AND BACK DOWN

Keep expanding your resources and take time to evaluate your existing research for clues you might have overlooked. Better yet, have someone else review it. Someone you've connected with on a blog or in a social media group. Keep building up a support group to help you make that trek up the mountain. These people understand your frustration over trying to determine if documents are fact or fiction, and they'll reinforce the need to go with your gut. They'll also tell you to ignore the skeptics who require information to be in black and white, because that will never happen. Gray is likely the closest you'll ever get.

Unable to locate another baptismal record for a James Watson in Chicago, I had to move forward with the belief that the one I had was my James's. My next big discovery was James Watson's parents' divorce papers. The document provided insight into his mother Bertha *Youngren* having fled an abusive marriage, then remarried and moved away. James was raised by his grandparents and likely never knew his mom or her maiden name, so provided a random surname, Conners, on his marriage record. Perhaps a Conners might pop up somewhere down the road as a family connection.

This James turned out to be an only child, so I was on to James III, the only sibling in his family to have children. Thanks to the census, I was off to Canada, online, to research James II and located his baptismal certificate, along with his two sisters', in Montreal. I encountered a few years up and down the mountain before I would get my next break, allowing me to reach Camp Three.

CAMP ONE TO CAMP THREE . . . AND BACK TO CAMP ONE

The big break that led to Camp Three was locating the military discharge papers for James Watson I, noting he was born in Pollokshaws, Scotland, circa 1811. Woot! I'd be sticking that Scottish flag in the summit in no time. I was on my computer and off to Scotland to find his baptismal record. I learned that Watson is one of the top twenty most common Scottish surnames. I found dozens of James Watsons born circa 1811 in the surrounding Glasgow area but not one in Pollokshaws. How could I choose one when I didn't know James's parents' names? The thin air at Camp Three, and a slight sense of defeat, had me trudging back down to Camp One for some much-needed oxygen. I had to clear my head, regroup, and have a glass of wine.

Research was now going much slower, and I needed to get more creative and dig deeper. I returned to Canada.

UP AND DOWN . . . UP AND DOWN . . .

James Watson II married Elizabeth Turney in Ontario, Canada, so I delved deeper into her family. The two families possibly had shared ties back to Scotland or Ireland—the birthplace of James's mother. I hired a genealogist who, after a failed attempt (back to Camp One) and my second request, located the marriage record for Elizabeth's parents and also a second marriage record for James Watson I. James's second marriage record provided the names of his parents. Revitalized, I was scurrying back up the mountain to Camp Four!

CAMP FOUR—SUMMIT IS IN VIEW . . . SNOWSTORM BLOWS IN . . . BACK TO CAMP ONE

After several unsuccessful weeks of searching online Scottish resources for the first James Watson's baptismal record or his parents' marriage record, I hired a genealogist in Glasgow to visit the archives. According to all the records I had, James was Presbyterian. When no records were found, the genealogist informed me that the family likely belonged to a Presbyterian descension church that had operated under the radar and hadn't kept records. Seriously? Flag in hand, I was feet from the peak of the mountain when this snowstorm blew in. This same thing happened to the keynote speaker, who had to make the difficult decision to push forward despite the storm or return to Base Camp. She was twelve feet from the summit, but at that high altitude, it took over a minute to make one step. Her goal within reach, she headed back down the mountain. She made it to the summit on future climbs.

I had no choice but to head back to Camp One, disheartened. I had my dad take a paternal Y-DNA test. My dad had no Watson matches, yet several dozen Burkes. I hadn't a clue what that meant. It wouldn't be until two years later that I determined my dad was biologically a Burke rather than a Watson. Double whammy. When and where had the surname changed, and was my research to date even valid? I'm currently back and forth between Camps One and Two analyzing my dad's DNA matches, trying to determine their connections and how they will all fit into this new family tree. His ethnicities also changed when Ancestry.com revamped their calculations. He's now more Norwegian and English and less Scottish. Who knows—when I finally reach the peak, I might be sticking a Norwegian or English flag in the ground!

WHERE ARE YOU AT ON THE MOUNTAIN?

If you find yourself saying, "I've done everything possible but still can't trace my ancestors," look at the underlying reason behind your mindset. If it's an assumption, and you truly believe you have done everything, then I'm telling you right now you're wrong. As I've mentioned previously, only 10 percent of genealogical documents are online. Even if you've researched off-line, you've likely only scratched the surface. Yet maybe you're tired of scratching, digging, and climbing . . . There is nothing wrong with coming to terms with the fact that it's time to move on. To put the research aside. You can always make the decision to return to it in the future. After all, your ancestors are dead. They aren't going anywhere.

MY JOURNEY FROM SOUTHWEST WISCONSIN, USA, TO COUNTY WESTMEATH, IRELAND

COFFEY FAMILY CASE STUDY

In my opening, "Becoming a Genealogist . . . How It All Began," I discussed my first Ireland trip in 2007 and the first family line I researched, the Dalys. Shortly after that time, I researched my Coffey ancestors. We knew as far back as my mother's great-grandfather, James Coffey, born circa 1860 in southwestern Wisconsin, who'd married Mary McDonald. According to family folklore, James's father—name unknown—had emigrated from Ireland. My goal was to trace the Coffeys back to their homeland.

This case study covers the research I conducted from 2008 to 2012. Thanks to binders and boxes packed with printed emails, written correspondence, and loads of documents, I was able to piece together my research process to the best of my recollection. Admittedly, my first time tracing a family backward rather than forward—like the Dalys—was overwhelming at times and a blur. It was also my introduction to the available US and Irish genealogical records and to Ancestry.com. Genealogy was just becoming in vogue, and there weren't many books yet published on the subject. Even if there'd been only *one*, I should have read it . . . a few times.

Thankfully, researching my Daly line forward had gone fairly smoothly. If I'd begun my genealogy endeavor with my Coffey line, I might have also *ended* it with that same line. The only family that has turned out to be as challenging—and possibly even more challenging—to research than my Coffey line, is my Watson line. At least they've both provided plenty of content and helpful hints for case studies. You can read about my Watson research next.

FALL/WINTER 2008

STEP ONE: US CENSUS

My first goal was to learn James Coffey's parents' names and if his father had emigrated from Ireland as family folklore had it. If I'd known James's death date or even the year, I might have tried to obtain his death certificate, which I'd assumed would have his parents' names. Because I didn't know his death date, I thought the easiest way to determine their names would be to locate the family in the 1860 US Census. Several relatives were fairly confident James had been born prior to that time and had grown up in southwest Wisconsin (three hours from where I had), where he'd later raise his family. I then thought I could piece together the entire family in no time at all. I laugh now at how naïve I was in the beginning.

When I couldn't locate the family in the 1860 census or any of the following ones, I wondered if James had grown up in Iowa or Illinois, but I couldn't find him there either. Finally I located a family with a two-year-old son, James, living in southwest Wisconsin with the last name Caffey. The spelling wasn't that far off from Coffey, yet I wasn't sure. (I eventually learned the benefit of utilizing "Soundex" and "Sounds Like" search options, which would have helped me locate this potential Coffey record much sooner. Ancestry.com's search engine has also become much better at detecting variations. If I now put in Coffey, Caffey comes up. Also, I should have created a family tree in the beginning so Ancestry.com would have automatically recommended other possible related records.) I couldn't be certain that Caffey was my Coffey family, but either name was an uncommon surname in the area at that time, and the family was close to where James would later live. At that point, I had to assume it was likely the correct family.

The census noted James's parents were Patrick and Margaret Coffey. Patrick was born in Ireland circa 1825. Yay! I had likely found my Coffey ancestor who'd emigrated. Margaret was ten years younger and had been born in Virginia. James had been born in Wisconsin, but had his parents married there or in Virginia? Patrick may have emigrated with his family as a young child and grown up on the East Coast. When I couldn't locate James's family in the following censuses, despite trying numerous spelling variations for Coffey, I wondered if they'd moved.

(I should have tried to locate the family by reviewing the original census document for the area where the family had lived in 1860. However, I doubt at that time I realized I could access the original rather than relying solely on the accuracy of the transcribed record.)

Now that I knew Patrick Coffey's name, I was off to find his death certificate, which would hopefully note his parents' names and his birth location in Ireland. And I needed a break from the frustration of unsuccessfully searching census records. I'd also searched the 1850 census for Patrick and his parents living in Virginia or Wisconsin and came up empty.

STEP TWO: DEATH CERTIFICATES

After a bit of research, I learned that the Wisconsin Historical Society's website had an index for birth, marriage, and death records dating mainly from 1880 to 1907. Wisconsin law required counties to register deaths with state officials starting in 1852, but the law was not strictly enforced until roughly 1880. When I was unable to find Patrick's death record, I wondered if that meant he'd died before 1880 or after 1907. Or had the record been filed incorrectly due to a misspelling, like in the 1860 census? Margaret's death record also wasn't on file. I was 0 for 2.

I figured the next best way to determine Patrick's death date was from his tombstone. Knowing when he'd died would enable me to locate his obituary, which likely noted his parents' names, his birth location, the name of every sibling . . . A girl could dream. First, I had to figure out where he was buried. All I knew at this point was where he'd lived in 1860.

STEP THREE: CEMETERY VISITS

While my parents were visiting relatives in southwest Wisconsin, they went to the cemetery near Patrick's home in 1860. According to my mom's uncle, the family had lived in that area for the duration of their lives. If he was correct, then why hadn't I located them in the censuses? Mainly Norwegian and German emigrants were buried at that cemetery. Patrick also wasn't buried in the next closest town.

When we later learned about a cemetery located a few miles west of the second town, my mom and I made another three-hour trek back over to southwest Wisconsin. This trip was a success! We located Patrick (b. 1825 d. 1873) and Margaret's (b. 1831 d. 1911) tombstone. No month and day were provided, but at least it was a starting point. And this confirmed that Caffey in the census was my Coffeys. Bonus: their son Michael (b. 1861 d. 1920) was buried next to them. Also, daughter Margaret, who'd died in 1879 at age ten, and a married daughter Catherine, who'd died in 1883 at age twenty-five.

I had mixed emotions. Discovering the tombstones was cause for celebration, yet how devastating that Margaret had lost her husband and two young daughters all within a ten-year period, 1873–1883. I would quickly learn that family research can often lead to some sad and disturbing discoveries. Michael Coffey had died merely nine years after his mother, Margaret. His elaborate tombstone was in pristine condition, same as his parents'. Michael had likely replaced Margaret and Patrick's tombstone, the newer one erected on top of the weathered remains of a previous stone. A stone that might have included the couple's birth locations like so many others in the cemetery. Oh well, at least I was leaving with death dates and the identity of three other family members.

I sent a letter to the parish priest requesting a burial record for Patrick, hoping it might contain his parents' names and birth location. It turned out the church had burned down along with all the records not long after Patrick's death. I would soon learn that churches, archives, libraries, and historical records depositories often went up in flames. Most buildings in Wisconsin being made of wood at that time were a fire hazard. (A relation of mine was a church caretaker and accidentally burned the church down.) The loss of the Coffeys' church also meant the loss of their children's baptismal records. On the upside, I would later discover that burial records merely contained cause of death, death date, and burial location.

Psyched about having Patrick's death year, I made plans to locate his obituary, hoping it would contain all his family background. Perseverance and optimism are necessary characteristics for a successful genealogist.

STEP FOUR: IRELAND BAPTISMAL RECORDS

Now that I had Patrick's birth year, the first thing I did when I returned home was search for his baptismal record in Ireland. I checked various spellings on Ancestry.com and FamilySearch to discover a handful of Patrick Coffeys born in 1825 in Ireland. Yet too many to know which was my Patrick. It was critical to learn his birth county or parents' names.

STEP FIVE: OBITUARY

The Coffeys lived in a rural area surrounded by five small towns, each of which published a newspaper. Thankfully, when I was on the website for the Wisconsin Historical Society, I recalled noticing that they boasted a large newspaper collection. Otherwise, I'd have had to visit each town's local library or historical society.

I made a two-and-a-half-hour road trip to the historical society to peruse the five newspapers on microfilm. The process was slower than expected due to tiny print that had to be magnified tenfold and no dedicated section for death announcements and obituaries. The items were placed wherever they fit best: front page, back page, and even in the middle of the ads section. After an entire day, I didn't once come across the name Coffey. Bleary eyed, disheartened, and desperate, I found myself hoping Patrick had died from a horrific farming accident that would have made the front page—but nothing.

I knew Margaret had died in 1911, but I wasn't keen on spending another day or two searching through papers and coming up empty. I needed to make more efficient use of the little research time I had between business trips. I visited the courthouse in the county where the couple had lived in 1860—still the only census I'd located them in. Maybe Margaret's obituary would contain information about Patrick's death, children, and more. And maybe I'd come across Patrick's death certificate at the courthouse. Maybe it had been overlooked by the historical society, or the local courthouse had failed to forward it to the state. A lot of maybes.

STEP SIX: COURTHOUSE VISIT AND OBITUARY

A few weeks later, and another tank of gas, the records clerk at the local courthouse informed me that neither Patrick's nor Margaret's death record was on file. What happened to the mandatory filing of vital records? She died forty years after Patrick. Why wasn't a simple piece of paper filed documenting her death when a massive tombstone had been erected? Again disheartened, and a bit cranky, I stopped at the local historical society and reviewed their 1911 newspaper on microfilm. Thankfully, in the forty years since Patrick had died, the paper now had larger print and the layout was much more organized, making the paper easier to scan. I was just over halfway through the year when I came across an August obituary for the death of Margaret *Murtha* Coffey.

I seriously think I cried tears of joy.

At least someone had made the effort to write up a lovely obituary when they hadn't taken the time to file a death certificate. Margaret had died at the age of seventy-nine years, seven months, and five days. Born in County Wicklow, Ireland, not Virginia as noted in the 1860 census, she'd come to America at age two with her parents. The family had settled in Maryland Heights, Maryland, for twelve years before moving to Wisconsin.

(FYI, I later learned after much research that Maryland Heights is in Missouri. Who knew? Once having this key piece of information, I checked ship manifests for the family having arrived into the port of New Orleans, rather than an eastern seaport, like Baltimore, *Maryland*. They'd quite possibly traveled up the Mississippi River from New Orleans to Maryland Heights, located a short distance from the important waterway. Unfortunately, this great clue didn't lead to me finding the family on a ship manifest.)

Had the Murtha family known the Coffeys in Ireland and Patrick was also from County Wicklow? The obituary noted the couple's wedding date. Hopefully, their marriage certificate would give their parents' names. I'd finally caught a break, and the couple had been married at a different church than the one that had burned down. At least I hoped that church hadn't also been destroyed. It listed three out-of-town funeral guests and that five out of nine of Margaret's children were still living. I knew from the tombstones two who'd died, but who were the other two? At least it provided the names of five living sons.

I now had numerous leads to follow. However, it would be almost a year later that I'd discover a major clue I'd overlooked in the obituary. Maybe I'd been so overwhelmed with all the obvious clues that one of the most critical pieces of information hadn't jumped out at me. Stay tuned for further details . . .

I regrouped and evaluated how to proceed, fingers crossed that the marriage certificate included Patrick's parents' names. I also had to go back to the dreaded census to finish piecing together all of Patrick and Margaret's children, including the other two who'd died but weren't buried by the family. And maybe I could find Patrick's and Margaret's families living in Wisconsin in the 1850s census prior to the couple's marriage in 1854. I'd been dabbling in the census during this time, but now it was time to get serious in my search.

STEP SEVEN: TRYING TO STAY FOCUSED

While conducting my Coffey research, I often found myself venturing off in different directions. After learning that Margaret Coffey's maiden name was Murtha, I searched for her family in County Wicklow and found baptismal records for her and a sister, Rose. Even though I told myself I should be researching the Coffeys not the Murthas, I'm glad I didn't listen. It turned out one of the couple's children who'd died had been named Rose. Knowing this daughter had been named after Margaret's sister would later help when I pieced the tree together based on the traditional Irish family naming pattern, which I will touch on shortly.

Also knowing James Coffey had married a Mary McDonald, I found myself dabbling in McDonald family research, which then led to Butler research when I discovered Eliza Butler had been Mary's mother . . . My mind was like a ping-pong ball. I was all over the place. I would have to keep reining in my curiosity that wasn't directly related to the Coffey research. Yet you just never know what will end up being related and what won't. Like the fact that I'd soon discover the Butlers and McDonalds had also been from County Wicklow. Interesting . . .

STEP EIGHT: OBTAINING MORE RECORDS

At long last I located the Coffeys in the 1870 census—their last name had been transcribed incorrectly as Coppe. During all this searching, I learned the importance of reviewing the original census document. From the 1860 to the 1910 census, the name was never spelled the same way twice due to errors in transcription or the original recording by the census enumerator. Often it was the case that the person themself couldn't spell their own name, but I later knew from Patrick's naturalization papers that he could spell his name. In 1880 the name was spelled Coffee. In 1900 it was Cooley. In 1910, a year before Margaret's death, it was finally spelled correctly! There are so many surname errors in early census records that I usually search by the family member with the most unique first name or birth location. However, that's a bit difficult when most Irish families at that time had a James, John, Patrick, Mary, and a Bridget.

The 1880 census had Margaret's birthplace as Maryland. The woman had now been born in Virginia, Ireland, and Maryland—or possibly *Missouri*, since I now knew the actual location of Maryland Heights. There was so much conflicting information that it was difficult to know what was correct. Patrick or Margaret would have provided the 1860 census information and Margaret the 1880 census. However, a distraught loved one not thinking clearly would likely have given her birthplace as County Wicklow in her obituary. Experience has taught me that more reliable information is provided by a person themself rather than by a family member. Not in this case. Once again, it was a good thing that I'd veered off track and found Margaret's baptismal certificate in County Wicklow even though I was technically researching the Coffey line.

I contacted the church where Patrick and Margaret were wed and offered to make a nice donation in exchange for a copy of their marriage record. I crossed my fingers that church hadn't met the same fate as the other one. I anxiously waited to hear back from the priest. And waited . . . and waited.

Next, I researched what other documents might give a birth location and parents' names. If I could narrow down the county where Patrick was born, I could revisit Ireland's baptismal records. I learned that naturalization records were my best bet for obtaining a person's birth location, even though it was hit or miss for that time period what information would be included. Immigrants generally applied for citizenship to obtain the right to vote and to acquire free land through homesteading. Naturalization papers were on file at an area archive in Platteville, four hours away in southwest Wisconsin. I booked a hotel room and prepared for my genealogy road trip.

SPRING 2009

STEP NINE: NATURALIZATION RECORDS, PLAT MAPS, TAX ROLLS, AND MORE

I visited the historical record depository in Platteville with the goal of obtaining Patrick's naturalization record. I carefully sifted through hundreds of original, delicate tissue-paper sheets before discovering his Declaration of Intention—renouncing his allegiance to foreign governments—filed in May 1852 at the age of twenty-five. (If correct, that would mean he was born in 1826 or 27, not 1825 as permanently engraved on his tombstone.) In July 1851, he'd arrived into the Port of New York. Most importantly, he'd been born in County Westmaid (Westmeath). Bingo! I'd narrowed down his birth county in Ireland from thirty-two to one. I could now figure out which of the handful of baptismal records was for my Patrick. No other Coffey naturalization papers for that same time period provided leads for possible family members.

FYI, I never did locate the ship manifest despite having Patrick's arrival information. At that time the only details recorded on a manifest were a person's name—often misspelled—approximate age, ethnicity, and departure port. A lot of Patrick Coffeys had arrived in

New York in July 1851. Once Ellis Island opened in 1892, researching arrivals became much easier thanks to more legible and standardized records.

During my archives visit, I sat at a table with a large map displayed under a glass top. I learned this was an 1860s Wisconsin plat map that detailed land ownership boundaries. The owner's name was written on the land parcel, giving you a visual of your ancestor's homestead and the surrounding neighbors. This was a great discovery. Since then I've often used plat maps in my research to determine my ancestors' neighbors, which I then researched. Immigrants tended to relocate near people from their homeland. Of course, that wasn't the case with my Coffeys, who'd lived in an area populated mostly by Norwegians and Germans.

The archivist introduced me to tax rolls, which recorded when the Coffeys had purchased the land, the number of acres, and the value. According to the 1865 tax roll, they'd leased rather than owned land. Sometime between 1865 and 1872 they purchased their 80-acre farm, valued at $340 in the 1872 tax roll, and they also owned 60 acres in a bordering township, valued at $380. At the time of his death in 1873, Patrick died owning 140 acres, valued at $720. When his father, James, died in 1876 in Ireland, he still *leased* 30 acres from an English landowner, never having owned the land he'd worked so hard on his entire life. James would have nothing to pass on to his children except for livestock and farm equipment. This made a great addition to the family bio I was compiling.

FYI, in the 1880s tax roll, the land was in Margaret's name, meaning Patrick had died. Tax rolls can be a great resource for learning unknown death dates.

The second most important clue I discovered that trip was that the archivist assisting me had previously helped someone else researching the same family. Her notes showed that she'd obtained Margaret's death certificate from the county courthouse. Wasn't that interesting considering I'd been told there wasn't one on file? Guess I'd be paying that courthouse another visit.

SUMMER/FALL 2009

STEP TEN: IRELAND BAPTISMAL RECORDS

Now knowing that Patrick was from County Westmeath, I revisited the baptismal records on Ancestry.com for the handful of Patrick Coffeys born in 1825. Not one had been born in Westmeath. Based on the age given on Patrick's naturalization papers, he'd been born in 1826 or 1827. No Westmeath baptismal records for those years either. I checked two years prior to 1825 and found one Patt Coffey born in 1824 in Westmeath. Having discovered Roots Ireland, a site offering a larger collection of records, I checked it out but still only found that one 1824 baptismal record for Westmeath.

That had to be my Patrick, right? Seriously, what was the chance it wasn't? Fairly good . . .

STEP ELEVEN: LOCATING MARGARET'S DEATH CERTIFICATE

I returned to the local county courthouse to once again inquire about Patrick's and Margaret's death certificates. This time the clerk allowed me to review the index myself. Now knowing Margaret's death date, a name immediately jumped out at me. Margaret Caffy, rather than Coffey, close to the Caffey misspelling in the 1860 census. The clerk had overlooked a spelling similar to the actual name. Even experts make mistakes. Something I would need to keep in mind with future research. However, despite searching every possible spelling over a ten-year period, I didn't locate a death record for Patrick. I purchased a copy of Margaret's death certificate. In the end, the other information except her mother's first name was correct.

By now I had Margaret's death certificate, obituary, tombstone picture, Irish baptismal record for her *and* her sibling, Rose, Irish marriage record for her parents, Michael and Catherine (still was waiting on Patrick and Margaret's marriage record), and a burial record for her father, Michael Murtha (recorded as Murtagh), whose tombstone was no longer in existence. Pretty much the only thing I hadn't located for the Murtha family was if they'd had a dog licensed in Ireland in the early 1800s.

All I knew about Patrick was that he'd likely been born sometime between 1824 and 1827 and had died in 1873, unless his tombstone possibly had both his birth and death years wrong. He'd been born in County Westmeath, unless the person recording the information on his naturalization papers had misinterpreted his thick Irish accent and heard *Westmaid* when he'd actually said *Wexford*. Almost a year after beginning my research, the only thing I knew for certain was that Patrick Coffey had to have had *two* parents.

I just needed to know their names.

STEP TWELVE: DISCOVERING AN OVERLOOKED CLUE AND MY FIRST BIG BREAK

While comparing the information on Margaret's death certificate to her obituary, seeing the couple's wedding date reminded me that it'd been over six months since I'd requested their marriage record and still no response. It was time to step it up. I reached out to a distant cousin, a nun in Minnesota, and kindly asked her to follow up. She was happy to assist. If she couldn't get a copy of a church record, I certainly never would.

Something else in the obituary sparked my curiosity. Who were the out-of-town funeral guests from Davenport, Iowa, and Richard Coffey from Missouri? I'd originally assumed Richard was a grandson of Margaret's. Since then I'd pieced together the children's families, and Margaret did indeed have a grandson Richard. However, he would have been thirteen years old when his grandmother had died. He wouldn't likely have been living that far from his family and traveling up on his own from Missouri. Was he

Patrick's brother, nephew, or cousin? And who were the two women from Iowa identified merely by their husbands' names?

I anxiously checked the 1910 census and found three Richard Coffeys approximately the same age living in Missouri, one of whom had been born in Illinois. The state borders Wisconsin, twenty miles south of Patrick's home, so I pursued this Richard. In 1870 a Richard lived with his father, Michael Coffey, in Davenport, Iowa, the same place the two women funeral attendees were from. Michael, born in Ireland, would have been about the same age as Patrick, so likely a brother or first cousin. The census also provided the first names of Michael's daughters. These names combined with their husbands' last names from the obituary helped me locate the couples' marriage records online. The women's father was . . . Michael Coffey.

I nearly fainted from excitement!

Now, I needed to determine Michael's relation to Patrick. I traced Richard and his two sisters' families forward and contacted several descendants. While waiting anxiously for a response, I obtained as much information as possible about Michael Coffey.

Lesson learned that out-of-town funeral attendees can be important clues. Even if I'd wrongly assumed Richard was a grandson, I should have researched the two women from Davenport. I'd been unknowingly sitting on a critical clue for nearly a year. I was upset, but I needed to give myself a break. I was still learning, albeit the hard way, but I was learning . . .

WINTER/SPRING 2010

STEP THIRTEEN: CORRESPONDING WITH NEARBY DISTANT RELATIONS

Michael Coffey's great-granddaughter replied to my letter. Her family had no knowledge of a Patrick Coffey from Wisconsin. However, they knew the name of the small town in Westmeath where Michael had been born in September 1835. For the privacy of all involved, I'll call the rural town Coffeyville. Yes! The county on the naturalization papers had been correct, and I now also knew the town where Patrick had likely been born. If he was indeed Michael's *brother*.

I checked Ancestry.com and Roots Ireland for Michael Coffeys born in 1835 in Westmeath. Not one. However, there was one born in 1833 and 1834, but neither were in September. You'd think either his birth month or year would be correct. Every step forward seemed like two steps back. Like climbing Mount Everest.

I reminded myself that all records weren't online, so I shouldn't feel defeated. I contacted genealogist Jane Daly, who'd assisted me with my Dalys research. She reviewed the original baptismal registers at the National Archives in Dublin and found a Michael Coffey born in September 1832 in Coffeyville. Correct month and town, but wrong year for the Michael in Davenport, Iowa. Jane explained that the Irish rarely knew their birth year and were much more likely to know the month and a day close to the actual date. She'd also checked for my Patrick's baptismal record but had come up empty. If he'd been the firstborn, she said his mother would have gone home to her parents for the birth. If I couldn't confirm where *Patrick* had been born, how would I ever figure out his mother's hometown?

Without Patrick's baptismal record, I couldn't confirm his relationship to Michael.

This was around the time Jane told me about the traditional Irish naming pattern discussed in Tip 3. One of the most important tips I've learned to date. So important that I will explain it once again in a nutshell.

The Irish traditionally adhered to a family naming pattern until the early 1900s. The first son was named after the father's father. The second son after the mother's father. The third son after the father. The fourth son after the father's oldest brother. The fifth son after the father's second oldest brother, and so on down the line through a dozen plus kids. The daughters were named in the same pattern after the maternal side of the family. It's critical to know where in order each child was born, both living and dead. When a child died, his or her name was often used again for the next-born son or daughter. This demonstrates just how important it was to pass down family names and how confusing it can get for genealogists. The naming pattern isn't an exact science. If the pattern resulted in a duplication of names, such as both grandfathers having had the same name, then the parents skipped to the next name on the list. Personal reasons also came into play. A mother might not have wanted to name a child after her abusive father.

Michael Coffey had been born in Coffeyville to a James Coffey and Mary Flanagan. Based on the naming pattern, my Patrick's parents would also have been James and Mary. Even though I knew eight of Patrick and Margaret's nine children, I'd been unable to locate one of the deceased children mentioned in Margaret's obituary. That child's name would alter the naming pattern as I knew it. And back then there were likely more James and Marys than there were sheep in Ireland.

I needed to somehow confirm Patrick and Michael's relationship.

STEP FOURTEEN: A BIT OF GOSSIP

While searching for obituaries from the late 1800s and early 1900s, I'd often been sucked into reading a newspaper's gossip column, giving insight on who was doing what with whom and where, and possibly why. Like maybe the Coffeys had recently traveled to Davenport, Iowa, for their *uncle* Michael's funeral?

The next time I had a few weeks between business trips, I visited the Wisconsin Historical Society and checked out twenty-five rolls of microfilm for the local newspapers from that time period. James Coffey and his four brothers had spread out a bit from where they'd grown up, so I had to determine which newspaper was recording the juicy details about my ancestors' lives. Knowing Michael Coffey's death date, when I still didn't know Patrick's, it took merely a few hours when I came across a snippet about the Coffey boys having been to Davenport to visit their "uncle" Michael Coffey, who'd been deathly ill. Yay!

Yet knowing that newspapers sometimes printed incorrect info, especially in a gossip column, I needed to find one more instance referencing their "uncle." Also, I'd been obtaining a lot of fun family facts while perusing the columns. For example, *James Coffey and family take solid comfort riding in a two-seated carriage recently purchased off Blanchard Bros.* The editor was making the best use of the paper's available space by slipping an ad in with the personals. It took more time, but I finally came across another mention of *Uncle* Michael three years earlier when he had been up from Davenport visiting his *nephews.*

That was enough to convince me that Patrick and Michael had indeed been brothers. Even if Patrick hadn't been born in Coffeyville, he'd grown up there, along with his brother and parents, James and Mary. I think I drank a pint of Guinness in celebration that evening!

STEP FIFTEEN: A MARRIAGE RECORD . . . FINALLY!

Thanks to my cousin the nun and a new priest at the church where Patrick and Margaret were wed, I finally received their marriage record. Sadly, it wasn't worth the effort and long wait. The only new information it contained was the two witnesses' names. I never did find a connection between them and the married couple. At least I was no longer wondering what clues the record *might* hold. And this is where I realized the importance of documenting sponsors and witnesses, which were often family members or friends.

STEP SIXTEEN: PREPARING FOR AN IRELAND TRIP

Having confirmed that Patrick and Michael were brothers, I was psyched to visit my ancestors' hometown. Over the past year, I'd been corresponding with a newfound Daly relative, Charlotte, in Ireland. I was now motivated to locate Coffey relatives to also visit on the trip. I pieced together more of Patrick's siblings so I could trace them forward and find descendants of those who'd remained in Ireland rather than immigrating to America.

FALL 2010, TRIP TO IRELAND!

STEP SEVENTEEN: VISITING IRELAND'S CEMETERIES

Unfortunately, despite months of rigorous research, I was unable to locate any living Coffey relations to visit during our trip to Ireland. I'd have to settle for dead ones, who might not even be related. My Daly cousin Charlotte's mother-in-law worked with a Matthew Coffey, who lived ten miles south of Coffeyville. I was convinced that he must at least be a distant relation. He was aware of an old cemetery in his area with numerous Coffey graves and offered to take us there during our visit.

We never would have found this cemetery located down a remote one-lane road without that kind gentleman. The cemetery surrounded an abandoned medieval church, where I envisioned my ancestors having attended Mass two hundred years earlier. We had to traverse long grass and uneven ground to reach three ivy-covered tombstones enclosed within a leaning wrought iron fence. Outside the fence were two additional weathered Coffey tombstones that could only be read when the sunlight hit them at just the right angle. Thankfully, the rain held off and sunshine filled the cemetery.

Each of the five tombstones recorded family history going back to the early 1700s. A feat that could never have been accomplished searching Ireland's archives for months because of the number of historical documents destroyed in a 1922 fire. I'm not certain if all family members noted were buried there, but that would account for the uneven ground and dirt mounds. We stripped ivy from the front of a lead-engraved stone and learned that a Christopher Coffey, who died in 1824, had played an integral role in the Rebellion of 1798. A sense of pride welled up inside me even though I had no clue if he'd been a relation. With everyone's assistance, including the sun's, I managed to transcribe all five stones. I was a bit disappointed to find a James and Polly on a stone, but no James and Mary, Patrick and Michael's parents. But it was interesting seeing the family naming pattern put into practice going back four to five generations. Each stone memorialized numerous family members, including several women's maiden names.

During that trip, we also visited the Coffeyville cemetery, which unfortunately had all newer graves. However, while we were there, we met a nice man who took us to a remote cemetery in the middle of a sheep field that, once again, we'd never have found by ourselves. It turned out his name was Gavaghan, possibly a relation—Patrick's sister Catherine had married a Gavaghan.

My fourth-great-aunt Catherine Coffey Gavaghan had been watching over us that day.

STEP EIGHTEEN: FAMILY GATHERING

Charlotte's mum, Jean, held a family gathering at her home in County Wicklow. The Daly relatives came down from Belfast and joined us. I was able to personally thank Charlotte's mother-in-law for putting us in touch with Matthew Coffey. Charlotte's father-in-law, Franz, and I spent time discussing our passion for genealogy. Coincidentally, he had family that had emigrated from Ireland to Galena, Illinois, just an hour from my ancestors in southwestern Wisconsin. I offered to assist him with research.

I was returning home psyched not only to conduct further research on my family but also to help others with all the knowledge I'd gained over the past three years.

JANUARY 2011

STEP NINETEEN: CLUES FROM AN IRISH HISTORIAN

After I arrived back home, I researched Franz's family in Galena, which I traced to Chicago, and eventually put him in contact with a living relative in California. During that same time, Franz had been speaking with a local historian who put him in touch with a historian in the Coffeyville area. The gentleman had transcribed all the surrounding cemeteries and baptismal and marriage records in the churches. He sent me what information he had on the Coffey families, which provided several new leads for a few of Patrick's siblings.

The list of baptisms for the area showed my James Coffey and Mary Flanagan had eight children and a James Coffey and Polly Flanagan had two children. Interesting that what were likely two cousins had married sisters. I recalled having seen James and Polly's grave on my recent trip to Ireland. If these two couples were indeed related, I still held out hope that we were somehow connected to the family in that medieval cemetery.

APRIL 2011

STEP TWENTY: MAJOR BREAKTHROUGH

That April I received another letter from my new historian friend in Ireland, including some additional transcriptions. He also noted that on the previous information he'd sent that two of the families recorded had actually been one family. *Mary* Flanagan had also been recorded as *Polly* Flanagan. I hadn't a clue that Polly was a nickname for Mary. (See Tip 28 about some of the unusual nicknames I've come across.) I was ecstatic to say the least! I was directly related to that incredible Coffey cemetery plot and had *my* family traced back to the early 1700s. And I was now even prouder of Christopher

Coffey's role in the Rebellion of 1798. In the end, Patrick and Margaret having strictly adhered to the traditional family naming pattern had been instrumental in me successfully tracing their line.

AND THE STORY CONTINUES . . .

I would go on to discover much more information on my Coffey family and to find a living Coffey descendant, Bernard, with whom we have spent many memorable occasions. If you haven't already, you can read about my journeys to discover living relatives and family homesteads in Tips 48 and 49.

Next, there are still a few of Patrick's siblings I've been unable to trace forward and will continue trying to do so and to locate more living relations in Ireland. So in conclusion, my Coffey family research will never *conclude*.

Discovering our Coffey graves thanks to Matthew Coffey

Our Coffey family's grave plot in County Westmeath, Ireland

Patrick and Margaret Coffey's five sons in Wisconsin, circa 1900

FROM TYPE B BLOOD TO BLUE BLOOD: HOW A PATERNAL DNA TEST CHANGED MY LINEAGE

WATSON FAMILY CASE STUDY

In 2018, prior to taking a trip with my parents and sister Sandra to our Watsons' homeland, Scotland, I had my dad take a paternal Y-DNA test. I was anxious to locate Watson relations for us to meet on our trip. This test can only be taken by a male in the family. A male's Y chromosome is passed down from father to son virtually unchanged for thousands of years. How could I not find some Watson relations?

The test resulted in only thirty-eight male matches. It turned out a Y-DNA test isn't nearly as popular as the autosomal DNA test because it's quite costly and has a much smaller database. Even more surprising was the variety of surnames, including numerous Burkes, but not one Watson. I knew that some matches and my dad's MRCA could go back hundreds of years before the time of standardized surnames. (See Tip 38 for more information on surnames.) But 50 percent with the last name Burke? Had a Burke reunion inspired family members to take Y-DNA tests? I decided it may take time for Watson matches to test. Far from a DNA expert, I didn't know where to begin trying to determine the matches' connections.

So I didn't.

Two years later, I was frustrated that traditional research still hadn't enabled me to break down my Watsons' brick wall. I upgraded my dad's test to FamilyTreeDNA's Big Y-700 test. The upgrade cost about $250. The test's name alone gave me high expectations and confidence that this would be just what I needed to finally trace my Watsons back hundreds of years. The test once again resulted in over 50 percent Burke matches but not one Watson. I was baffled. Then the light slowly flickered on in my head.

Were we not biologically *Watsons*? Were we *Burkes*?

How could that have happened?

Needing emotional support and DNA guidance, I reached out to fellow members on a Watson Y-DNA forum at FamilyTreeDNA.

STEP ONE: THE COLD, HARD FACTS

I'd joined the Watson forum two years earlier when my dad had taken the first paternal test. After his test resulted in zero Watson matches, I never returned to the site. If only I had, instead of waiting two years for Watson matches to materialize, I might be writing a completed case study rather than one in progress.

The general consensus from forum members was "Congratulations! You're a Burke!"

I hadn't felt the least bit like celebrating.

I'd been so attached to my Watson surname that I'd kept my maiden name after being married. I'd spent years and thousands of hours researching the Watson line and visiting our family's homeland in Scotland. Was my research tracing the line back to our ancestor James Watson, born 1811 in Scotland, even accurate? I'd become emotionally attached to each one of the 452 relatives in my Watson family tree. I couldn't imagine having to delete any of them. Despite numerous setbacks and disappointments in my thirteen years as a genealogist, I'd always managed to suck it up and continue on. Until that moment. I guarantee I had more than one glass of wine that evening.

After spending several days trying to recover from the shock, I was still unsure if I should share my discovery with my family. Yet what happened to my genealogist code of ethics, that everyone had a right to know the truth? I'd uncovered my biggest family secret to date and was considering keeping it to myself? I called my sister Sandra with my ethical dilemma. She convinced me to pursue what I'd discovered and go where the DNA led me. In the end I could decide whether or not to share the test results, but she thought I should. I'd likely confided in her foreseeing her reaction and reinforcing what I knew deep down was the right thing to do.

STEP TWO: GOODBYE WATSON CLAN AND HOWDY BURKES

I joined a Burke Y-DNA forum where members welcomed me with open arms. Fifty percent of them also had a non-Burke surname as the result of an NPE. That was the first time I'd heard the term NPE, which included numerous possibilities for how our surname had changed from Burke to Watson at some point in history.

1. An adoption of a Burke child by a Watson couple.

2. A Burke father died, and his wife remarried a Watson.

3. An out-of-wedlock birth occurred, and the mother's Watson family surname was given to the child.

4. An infidelity—known or unknown to the family.

5. A male assumed an alias to elude the law or for another reason. (See Tip 38 on surnames. The poor MacGregors in Scotland had to renounce their surname or be executed.)

The forum's administrator and DNA expert estimated that my dad and his closest Y-DNA match, who also has a non-Burke surname, shared an MRCA circa the 1600s in England. What a relief. The further back the better. It would make breaking the news to my dad a bit easier than if it'd occurred in the last generation or two. And it gave me hope that my traditional research was accurate back to our James Watson born 1811 in Scotland. All those relatives could continue hanging out in our family tree. For now, anyway.

I learned that based on our haplogroup—people who share a common paternal or maternal ancestor that determines their ancestry origin—we are descended from Richard Óg de Burgh, second Earl of Ulster. Richard's granddaughter Elizabeth married Robert the Bruce, king of Scotland—portrayed in the movie *Braveheart*—and she became Queen of Scots. Robert the Bruce led, and won, the war against England for Scottish independence.

A sense of pride rose inside me. Our family had a connection with the most famous figure in Scottish history, instrumental in changing that country's future. This helped lessen the blow of not biologically being a Watson. The only way I could have been more thrilled was if we were related to Sir William Wallace, played by Mel Gibson in *Braveheart*. William Wallace was a Scottish knight and one of the country's greatest heroes who fought for Scotland's freedom. If I hadn't seen *Braveheart*—even though my eyes were closed through half the violent movie—I wouldn't have realized the magnitude of this discovery.

STEP THREE: CONTACT MY DAD'S CLOSEST Y-DNA MATCHES

The first gentleman I reached out to had the last name Burke. His earliest known ancestor was born in 1800 in Loughrea, County Galway, Ireland. The town is located just south of Tuam, where the second man's earliest known ancestor was born in 1740. These dates were much later than my dad's connection to his closest match estimated circa 1600. Historically, the Burke clan had a strong presence in County Galway, where they'd spent hundreds of years building 121 castles. Still, bells were going off in my head because of the Loughrea and Tuam locations.

Prior to our Scotland trip, I'd also been researching my dad's Irish ancestors. On a whim—and out of desperation—I'd searched for a

James Watson born in Ireland. After all, there'd been a lot of travel back and forth between Scotland and Ireland's Ulster province at that time, and we had ties to Counties Antrim and Down just across the pond from Scotland. I came across a baptismal record for a James Watson born in 1811 to a John and Barbara Watson in Tuam, County Galway.

My James's parents were also James and Barbara (Neil). In Scotland, John had been a popular nickname for James, and my James was later recorded as John in city directories. (I'll continue to refer to this potential father as John to lessen the confusion between James Sr. and James Jr.)

This James's baptismal record noted John was a soldier in the Donegal Regiment. Loughrea was a major military garrison at that time where John Watson would have been stationed. Enlisted in Her Majesty's Military, John had most likely been from Scotland or England. Actually, I should have considered the possibility much sooner that my James may have followed in his military father's footsteps and could have been born anywhere in the world.

Interestingly, the baptisms registered in that area only noted the father's occupation if he'd been in the military. Likely because the clergymen wouldn't have personally known the men, not having been locals. Even more interesting, only *eight* Watson baptisms were registered in County Galway from 1800 to 1820. All were Roman Catholic, except for one. John and Barbara Watson's son James was baptized in the Church of Ireland—Protestant. Being Scottish, my ancestors were Presbyterian. However, Presbyterian churches were rare in a county that was 95 percent Roman Catholic. Non-Catholic worshippers would have attended the Church of Ireland.

According to several historical records, our James's mother, Barbara Neil, was Scottish. However, Neil is a much more common Irish surname, and the majority of my dad's autosomal DNA matches' Neils, O'Neils, and McNeils are Irish. The best candidate I've found for our Barbara in Scotland lived in Glasgow. My dad has numerous DNA matches with the female surnames in this Barbara's line back a hundred years. However, he could connect to the surnames via other ancestors. I needed to consider the possibility that our Barbara was Irish and had married a Scottish military man, John Watson.

Despite DNA evidence that the NPE occurred much earlier than 1811, what was the chance that John Watson had been biologically a Burke from Scotland and years later ended up smack dab in the middle of his Burke ancestor's homeland? I've encountered plenty of coincidences in my research, which often makes it difficult to determine if something is a fact or merely a fluke.

This time, my gut leaned toward fluke.

Regardless, how was I going to best present our new de Burgh lineage to my dad when I couldn't confirm when, where, or how the surname change had occurred? Thanks to the assistance of several Watson and Burke DNA forum members, I came up with the most probable scenario.

A Watson female had a son fathered by a Burke man—possibly out of wedlock—who was adopted by a male Watson relation. Or the mother's Watson family surname was given to the child, who she raised. My dad has numerous DNA matches with Watson ancestors in their family trees. He has a strong connection to the surname Watson, which likely traces back in history to a Watson female.

STEP FOUR: RESEARCHING JAMES/JOHN AND BARBARA WATSON

I continued with some traditional genealogical research on John and Barbara Watson.

First, I had to determine if a John Watson from Scotland had been in the Donegal Regiment and stationed in County Galway, Ireland. This would help me verify the likelihood of it having been my James born 1811 in Tuam. I found one John Watson who met all the necessary criteria and is a possible candidate.

In 1786 a John Watson was born in Gorbals, Scotland, just

outside Glasgow, located less than two miles from Pollokshaws, my James's hometown.

In 1805 John enlisted in the 92nd (Gordon Highlanders) Regiment of Foot. A week later he was transferred to Birr, County Offaly, Ireland. Birr is located thirty miles from Loughrea, County Galway, the garrison city where a John Watson was stationed when his son James was baptized in 1811.

However, the father on the baptismal certificate was a soldier in the Donegal Regiment, not the 92nd Regiment of Foot like John from Gorbals. Had his regiment been recorded incorrectly? This is quite possible since there'd been numerous regiments stationed at the Loughrea garrison. Ordering a copy of the Donegal Regiment roster is on my to-do list.

John Watson from Gorbals, Scotland, had a twin brother, William. Later, a William Watson lived next to my James in Montreal, where he'd served in the military. My James named his son James William Watson, who would go on to name two sons William—reusing the name after the first son died. William was obviously an important family name. It may have come from James William's mother's line, whose father is unknown. However, his mother died when her children were young, and I've found no evidence that the children knew her father.

After John Watson from Gorbals retired from the military in 1841, he lived in Scotland with his wife, Ann (possibly a third wife he'd married in 1817), and a granddaughter. Come to find out, in 1803, two years before joining the military, John had married a Janet, and they had a daughter, Margaret. No records were found for additional children, and no death record for his wife, Janet, who seemed to have vanished. Having likely been a single father before enlisting in the military in 1805, John would have remarried, or his daughter would have lived with family in Gorbals, Scotland.

Second, I attempted to locate a marriage record for Barbara Neil and John Watson without success. They might have belonged to a Presbyterian descension church that didn't record events. However,

John from Gorbals hadn't belonged to one a few years earlier when marrying his first wife. Besides conducting online research, I hired a genealogist to review the original church registers in Glasgow, hoping the marriage had been recorded, just not transcribed. Unfortunately, no record was found.

Maybe Barbara had been married to a military man stationed at the Loughrea garrison who'd died. She'd then married John Watson. Ireland marriage records are a rare find for that time period. This could place an unmarried Barbara from Glasgow, Scotland, living in County Galway, Ireland. Or Barbara was indeed from Ireland but of Scottish descent. My dad has several DNA matches with Neils or McNeils from Londonderry, located near Letterkenny, where the Donegal Regiment was stationed.

Third, I couldn't find that John and Barbara Watson had additional children born anywhere in the world. I also haven't located her death information. This leads me to believe she'd died young when death recordings were inconsistent. Could poor John have been so unlucky to have lost two wives, Janet and Barbara, within a few years of each other? If Barbara had died, then her son James, born in Tuam, undoubtedly would have been raised by family in Pollokshaws while John Watson and his regiment fought in numerous famous battles, including Waterloo in the Napoleonic War.

In conclusion, the preceding evidence demonstrates that John and Barbara Watson, who baptized a son James in 1811 in Tuam, County Galway, are strong candidates for my ancestors. It'll require DNA evidence to confirm the theory. I am currently working with a descendant of John Watson and his first wife, Janet, in an attempt to locate possible shared DNA connections.

The week following my Burke discovery was a blur. Anxious for answers before talking to my dad, I was pulling all-nighters on Ancestry.com and living on SunChips and Diet Coke. Yet I was still holding off discussing this with my dad until I had more information or until I collapsed from exhaustion, too tired to conduct further research.

STEP FIVE: HOW FAR BACK COULD DNA CONFIRM THE RELATIONS IN OUR WATSON TREE?

Was the Watson family tree I'd compiled back to James Watson born 1811 in Pollokshaws, Scotland, or Tuam, County Galway, accurate? My dad's most recent DNA ethnicities reflect he's 10 percent Scottish, with the top ancestral location being Glasgow. I truly believe our Watsons were from Scotland but am unsure about the Neil line.

I'd confirmed DNA matches connected to my dad's paternal grandmother's German line and his great-grandmother's Swedish line. I was fairly confident about the DNA matches I'd linked to his second- and third-great-grandmothers' Irish lines. Thus, DNA evidence validated the line as I knew it back to James Watson born in 1811. However, when you go back further than five generations, the connections get iffy as to how they are related. That's why I like to have as much proof as possible.

It was important that I determined which ancestral line autosomal DNA matches shared in common with my dad. Ideally, I needed to group matches according to his sixteen second-great-grandparents. I then needed to weed out the matches connected to his eight maternal lines so I could focus on the eight *paternal* ones.

STEP SIX: LINKING DNA MATCHES TO ANCESTRAL LINES

In Tip 35 I discussed using a GEDmatch application that compares multiple matches at one time to help determine ancestral lines. It's called clustering. This application separates DNA matches into groups that cluster around one of your ancestral lines. I did overall clustering and also joined projects in Scotland and Ireland specific to locations and surnames, such as County Galway and the last names Burke and Neil.

Knowing the matches you share with another match is critical to determining a common connection. For example, if you and a DNA match have eight matches in common, and you all have the couple William and Biddy Molloy in your tree, you're most likely related through that couple or one of them.

When doing this clustering process, it's important that a close relation from each parents' lines has taken a DNA test to help establish a match's connection. You can then in turn use that close match to determine the connection of more distant shared matches. My dad has numerous first and second cousins from both sides of his mother's family. On his father's side, he has a fair number of cousins from his grandmother's German line and his great-grandmother's Swedish one. However, he's a third-generation only child in his Watson line, and his great-grandfather's siblings had no known offspring to produce descendants. The closest Watson match I can hope for is a third cousin, who'd have second-great-grandparents in common.

It's a good thing I'm always up for a challenge.

STEP SEVEN: MAPPING OUT COUNTY GALWAY DNA MATCHES

I mapped out my dad's DNA matches with County Galway connections in their family trees. I still believe the NPE occurred prior to our James's birth in 1811, yet wanted more insight into the Galway hotspot. There were over a hundred of these matches. Keep in mind, maybe 10 percent of my dad's matches even have family trees.

The first locations I marked on a map were for my dad's two Burke Y-DNA matches with earliest known ancestors born in Tuam and Loughrea. After plotting a dozen matches, I realized that not only were there Burke connections all over County Galway, but north into County Mayo and up into Sligo. And it was impossible to confirm if the connections in the matches' trees were through the Burkes or another Galway line. Based on the amount of shared DNA, most matches likely went back six or more generations to a possible common shared ancestor with my dad. When a match is that distant, Ancestry.com doesn't show your shared matches with that person. GEDmatch will show shared matches, but the further back you go, the less reliable.

Ireland's 1823–37 Tithe Applotment Books—a census substitute—listed 806 Burke households and merely five Watson ones, in County Galway. No wonder I was overwhelmed with Burkes. I redirected my focus to other surnames that kept popping up in my Galway research, like Love and McKee. I soon came across a Love who'd married a Watson just north of Galway in southern Donegal. And then another Love in that same townland had married a Watson. And then a McKee had married a Watson. Suddenly, three of the most common surnames I was researching were all intersecting within a one-mile radius and with a large cluster of Watsons. Same as the John and Barbara Watson in Tuam, they'd also belonged to the Church of Ireland. At that time Donegal was heavily populated by the English and Scottish.

Several years earlier I'd connected with a DNA match who was a McKee from Donegal. The MaGee/McKee surname had just come onto my radar. Our family had no known connection to either the surname or Donegal. I looked back at that DNA connection's tree. Bingo. His McKees came from the Donegal townland bordering on these Watson couples' town. They'd lived within a mile of each other. But how were they connected to my family? Or weren't they?

By now I was all over the Galway, Donegal, and Sligo maps. I was beginning to understand the meaning of low-confidence DNA and how it could connect you to geographic areas but not necessarily to ancestors. Most of these matches shared 8-15 cM, which could go back ten generations. James Watson b. 1811 in Scotland is back five generations, his parents six, so my dad would share an average of 8-15 cM with distant Watson relations. That is precisely why Y-DNA paternal testing is so important. It's a direct line back without female surnames muddying the connections. I'm still hoping a closer connection will materialize than the one who shares a MRCA circa 1600.

I stopped speculating and developing theories. Being a fiction author, my theories were endless. I needed to document what I knew for certain, or for almost certain. Otherwise, before long I'd be so overwhelmed with all the names, dates, and locations swirling around in my head that I wouldn't remember any of them.

First, I needed to present what little I'd confirmed to my dad.

STEP EIGHT: SURPRISE! WE'RE BURKES, NOT WATSONS!

I live two and a half hours from my parents. This was news that I needed to present in person, not over the phone. I caught up on sleep so I'd be in shape to make the drive and coherent enough to present the news. Not wanting to overwhelm him like I'd been for the past two weeks, I gave him a basic overview and information on some of the key de Burgh and other royal relations. Needless to say, same as me, he was shocked to learn that we were biologically Burkes rather than Watsons. At the same time, he was intrigued, being a big history and military buff. He was interested to see what additional family history I would uncover in the future.

So am I.

STEP NINE: ORGANIZING AND DOCUMENTING CONFIRMED DETAILS

Time to get organized. I created an Excel spreadsheet for tracking DNA matches. It includes the match's profile name, relationship (i.e., first cousin once removed), possible surname connections, locations, and notes. I also include the chromosome number on which they match. Unfortunately, at this time Ancestry.com doesn't provide the chromosome information, but other test sites do. I can sort by a surname and see where a cluster of that same name was located. And if a match's family tree has a Watson moving from Scotland to Ireland to America, I can include all three locations and cross-reference them to other matches whose ancestors had the same migration pattern.

I'm frequently analyzing GEDmatch clusters and chromosome browsers, adding those matches to the database to help determine shared ancestral lines between matches. At present I only have 784 entries in my database. I'd hoped to have thousands by now. However, it can take an hour to review one match's tree and identify possible surname connections. A tree can have anywhere from zero to twenty surnames to record.

Clustering is an extremely helpful yet time-consuming process. It is also an ever-evolving one. For example, my dad has a group of matches with the shared surnames Watson, Lynch, Knotts, Gregory, and a few others from Ireland and Scotland. I believed they were connected to a female in his Watson line. However, I recently learned my grandma Watson was not 100 percent Norwegian. Her maternal grandmother was English. One more line from the British Isle to throw into the mix. I needed to weed that line out. After much research I traced her English ancestors back to Lancashire and West Yorkshire. According to one DNA test site, these locations are my dad's third and fourth most likely ancestral regions in the UK. Bingo.

STEP TEN: START FISHING IN MORE THAN ONE POND

The GEDmatch clustering application is brilliant. However, I've only managed to determine matches for three of my ancestral lines. This is because analyzing the clusters is a slow process, and matches aren't responding to my emails. I uploaded my dad's DNA for free to My Heritage and FamilyTreeDNA and had him test at 23andMe. These were autosomal tests—testing both the maternal and paternal lines.

I recently received the results, but I can already see a major benefit to having my dad's test results on four major DNA sites plus GEDmatch. He now has his paternal and autosomal tests both on FamilyTreeDNA.

I can see autosomal matches who've also taken a Y-DNA test but don't match my dad through his male line. This is a huge help. If I rule them out as being from his mother's side, I'll know they match a female ancestor on his father's side and focus on determining their relations.

STEP ELEVEN: HIRE A PROFESSIONAL GENEALOGIST

No, I'm not feeling defeated and giving up. Remember, perseverance is a needed characteristic for a successful genealogist. However, I'm far from a DNA expert, and I feel overwhelmed. I need someone who is experienced in analyzing DNA. After laying all the groundwork, this will be the perfect time to hire a professional. Hopefully, she'll work her magic and pull a Burke out of her hat. I found the perfect candidate. She is a DNA expert based in Glasgow, a family hotspot, with a background in helping adoptees and others solve the mystery behind NPE. Everything I'm looking for in a genealogist.

STEP TWELVE: FUTURE RESEARCH . . .

Just because I'm hiring a professional genealogist doesn't mean I'll stop researching. The following are just a few of the items on my to-do list:

- Continue searching military records for possible John Watson candidates.
- Obtain the Donegal Regiment rosters to review information included on John Watson.
- Check on the availability of early 1800s school records for John's daughter Margaret in Gorbals and my James in Pollokshaws.
- Search cemetery transcriptions for a Barbara Watson buried in Ireland or Scotland.
- Continue hoping that my ancestors will reach out to me in my dreams . . .

- Add our early de Burgh relatives, and other royal relations, to our Watson family tree. There are loads of confirmed blue-blood connections to our family lineage that I haven't had time to focus on. Like Richard Óg de Burgh was descended from Richard the Lionheart, king of England. I'm beyond thrilled that these limbs of our family tree have already been researched and documented. Ah, yes, one of the benefits of having royal lineage.

- Purchase a small plot of land in a Scottish Highlands nature reserve to obtain my official Lady Eliza Watson title. And one day visit this property in my ancestors' homeland.

James Watson and Clara Burkart's wedding photo,
Milwaukee, Wisconsin, 1910

MY ANCESTORS' CAMEO
APPEARANCES IN MY NOVELS

I mentioned in the introduction that I'm thankful for being able to combine my two greatest passions, genealogy and writing. My personality, interests, and ancestors sometimes sneak into my novels without me realizing it, but usually it's intentional. The following are merely a few of the appearances my ancestors make in my two series, A Mags and Biddy Genealogy Mystery and The Travel Mishaps of Caity Shaw.

Every Irish surname in these series has a special connection to my ancestors, family, and friends. Caity Shaw's Irish grandmother, Bridget Coffey, and her newfound relative, Sadie Collentine, are named after my ancestors from County Westmeath. My third-great-grandmother Mary Murray, who emigrated from County Mayo, inspired the surname for character Mags Murray. Biddy McCarthy is named after my McCarthys. I have plenty of Bridget and Margaret ancestors, but these characters are specifically named for two good Irish friends who inspired the fun-loving amateur sleuths.

Caity's growing teacup collection began with a treasured cup from her Irish grandmother. Throughout her travels, Caity acquires cups that have a personal meaning to her. After my grandma passed away, I received part of her teacup collection. My latest addition is an antique cup and saucer purchased during a research trip to England. The cup and vintage shop play a role in Caity book 5.

Spring is my favorite time to visit Ireland, when all the lambs are born. Sheep decorate our home in Ireland, from salt and pepper shakers to a knitted teapot cozy and wall décor. Sheep make numerous appearances and play several significant roles throughout both series. I'm confident my ancestors raised sheep.

Ballycaffey, the fictitious town of quirky characters where Mags and Biddy live, is based on my Coffeys' hometown in County Westmeath. Mags inherits her grandmother's home, inspired by the 1887 renovated schoolhouse my husband and I purchased in that same townland in 2013. As I mentioned, several of our Coffey, Lynch, and Flanagan relations attended school at our home. We plan to one day retire there.

My Dalys' 1800s deserted home plays a role in both series. The book's description is true to the actual dwelling.

> My chest fluttering, I stepped onto the same land Grandma hadn't stepped foot on since leaving Ireland in 1936. Rusted metal sheets covered the deserted stone house's original thatched roof. Ivy trailed across the front and entered the dwelling through the glassless windows. A weathered green wooden door hung crooked on rusted hinges. And an outbuilding's stone roof lay in a pile of rubble in the middle of the crumbling structure.

I have explored more Irish graveyards than I can count. Many were located in the middle of sheep fields, at monastic ruins, or abandoned churches. I've traversed some rough terrain and even had my foot once slip into a sunken grave, which happens to poor Biddy. When visiting a cemetery at a medieval church, Caity feels a sense of pride over a tombstone memorializing my relative Christopher Coffey, who played a role in the Irish Rebellion of 1798.

You never know when or where my ancestors might appear in one of my novels . . .

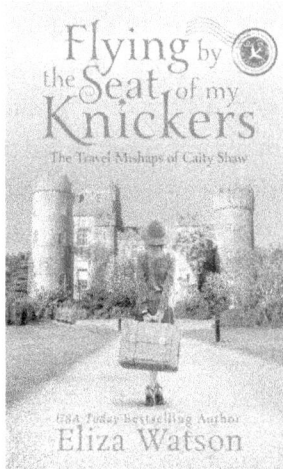

The Travel Mishaps of Caity Shaw

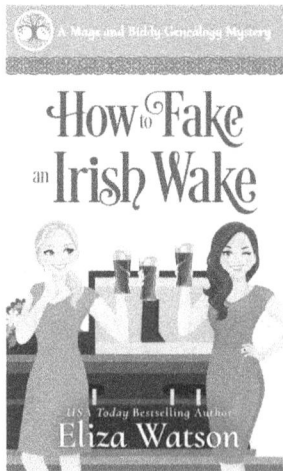

A Mags and Biddy Genealogy Mystery

GLOSSARY

The following are key terms used throughout the book. A detailed explanation can be found in the tip number provided.

autosomal DNA (atDNA) test: The test is used to find relatives on both your mother's and father's side of your family tree. (Tip 10)

Banns: An announcement in a couple's church, three Sundays in a row, of their intention to marry. (Tip 24)

census: An official count or survey of a population, typically recording various details of individuals, enabling you to track ancestors from decade to decade, location to location.

Church of Ireland: The Irish branch of the Anglican Church, the primary Protestant sect in England. The official state church in Ireland from 1690 to 1870, subject to parliamentary control. (Tip 20)

city directory: Prior to the telephone book, there was the annual city directory that listed a head-of-household name, address, profession, and in some cases ethnicity. The directory helps track the movement of people between the release of census records.

civil registration: The system by which a government records the vital events (births, marriages, and deaths) of its citizens and residents. (Tip 9)

cM: Centimorgans determine the amount of DNA you share with a match. The higher the cM number, the more closely related you are with the person. (Tip 35)

cousinhood: A relative descended from a common ancestor.

First cousins share grandparents. **Second cousins** share great-grandparents. **Third cousins** share 2nd-great-grandparents. (Tip 35)

Declaration of Intention: Prior to 1906, this was the first step in becoming a naturalized US citizen. (Tip 7)

emigration: The act of leaving *from* one's own country to settle permanently in another.

enumerator: A person employed to record a population census.

family naming pattern: Families often followed patterns for passing on given names from generation to generation. The traditions varied by country. (Tip 3)

Flax Report: The Irish Linen Board's 1796 Flax Growers List included 60,000 individuals, noting the person's name, parish, and county. A pre-1901 census substitute. (Tip 29)

forename: A person's given name, also known as a first name.

GEDmatch: A third-party online service with applications that compare your DNA results with matches from various testing companies, including Ancestry.com, FamilyTreeDNA, and 23andMe. (Tip 35)

genealogical DNA test: Genetic tests used to determine ancestral genealogical relationships or to estimate the ethnic mixture of an individual.

generation: A generation averages approximately twenty-five years from the birth of a parent to the birth of a child. (Tip 43)

Griffith's Valuation: A land and property document compiled in Ireland from 1847 to 1864 for the purpose of taxing leasers based on the properties' values. The most valuable pre-1901 census substitute. (Tip 47)

haplogroup: A group of people who have inherited common

genetic characteristics from the same most recent common ancestor going back several thousand years.

immigration: The act of coming *to* a foreign country to settle permanently.

mitochondrial DNA test (mtDNA): Mitochondrial DNA is passed down almost unchanged from a mother to her children, allowing a person to trace his or her maternal ancestry. Both males and females can take mtDNA tests. (Tip 10)

most recent common ancestor (MRCA): The ancestor who is shared by two or more individuals and was born most recently.

Northern Ireland: A region of the United Kingdom that occupies the northeastern part of Ireland, comprised of six counties of the Ulster province.

non-paternal event (NPE): Events or circumstances that cause a family surname to not match the family's bloodline. A surname change may have occurred somewhere in history due to an adoption, name change from a remarriage, or an infidelity. (Tip 38)

patronymic: A name derived from the name of a father or ancestor, typically by the addition of a prefix or suffix. (Tip 38)

Petition for Naturalization: Prior to 1906, this was the second step in becoming a naturalized US citizen. (Tip 7)

plat map: A map that shows land ownership boundaries delineated by tax parcel property lines. A plot is often labeled with the landowner's name, the square footage, the crop grown, and the number of dwellings. (Tip 18)

Republic of Ireland: A sovereign country in northwestern Europe occupying twenty-six of thirty-two counties of the island of Ireland.

Soundex: A system for coding and indexing family names based on the phonetic spelling of the name. (Tip 1)

surname: A person's family name, also known as a last name.

Tithe Applotment Books: The books were compiled in Ireland between 1823 and 1837 in order to determine the amount that occupiers of agricultural holdings over one acre owed in tax to the

Church of Ireland—the state church established under English rule. (Tip 47)

transcribe: To make a written copy of something, such as transcribing the inscription engraved on a gravestone.

Ulster: One of the four traditional Irish provinces located in the north of Ireland. It is comprised of nine counties. Six of these counties constitute Northern Ireland; the remaining three are in the Republic of Ireland.

Ulster Plantations: The organized colonization of Ulster by people from Great Britain during the reign of King James I. Most of the settlers were from southern Scotland and northern England and maintained a different culture from the native Irish. (Tip 20)

Y-DNA test: This test is used for tracing a person's paternal lineage and may only be taken by a male in the family. A male's Y chromosome is passed down from father to son virtually unchanged for thousands of years. (Tip 10)

WEBSITES

These are a few of the main websites referenced in the book. Please see individual tips for more websites and resources.

ANCESTRY.COM
Offers more than 20 billion names indexed from historical records.
www.ancestry.com

BILLIONGRAVES
A collection of gravesite photos, transcriptions, and memorials.
www.billiongraves.com

ELLIS ISLAND FOUNDATION
Over 65 million records for passengers arriving at the Port of New York from 1820 to 1957.
www.libertyellisfoundation.org/passenger

FamilySearch
Offers 7 billion searchable records and 3 billion unindexed images.
www.familysearch.org

Find a Grave
A collection of gravesite photos, transcriptions, and memorials.
www.findagrave.com

Findmypast
A UK-based service with over 4 billion searchable genealogical records.
www.findmypast.com

Fold3
The premiere online source for researching military records.
www.fold3.com

Random Acts of Genealogical Kindness
A database of volunteers donating their time to assist with genealogy research in their local area.
www.raogk.org

COFFEY & DALY FAMILY TREE

JAMES COFFEY
B. 1857 WISCONSIN

PATRICK COFFEY
B. 1825 COUNTY WESTMEATH, IRELAND

JAMES COFFEY
B. 1800 COUNTY WESTMEATH, IRELAND

MARY FLANAGAN
B. 1805 COUNTY WESTMEATH, IRELAND

MARGARET MURTHA
B. 1833 COUNTY WICKLOW, IRELAND

MICHAEL MURTHA
B. COUNTY WICKLOW, IRELAND

CATHERINE BROWN
B. COUNTY WICKLOW, IRELAND

JOHN COFFEY
B. 1889 WISCONSIN

JOHN MCDONALD
B. 1831 IRELAND

PATRICK MCDONALD (PENDING)
B. SCOTLAND

MARY KELLY (PENDING)
B. IRELAND

MARY MCDONALD
B. 1861 WISCONSIN

ELIZA BUTLER
B. 1836 COUNTY WICKLOW, IRELAND

MICHAEL BUTLER
B. COUNTY WICKLOW, IRELAND

ELEANOR BYRNE
B. COUNTY WICKLOW, IRELAND

EULALIA COFFEY (m. FRANCIS FLANNERY)
B. 1920 WISCONSIN

PATRICK DALY
B. 1858 COUNTY WESTMEATH, IRELAND

PETER DALY
B. 1830 COUNTY WESTMEATH, IRELAND

SARAH COLLENTINE
B. 1837 COUNTY WESTMEATH, IRELAND

MICHAEL COLLENTINE
B. IRELAND

SALLY FLYNN
B. IRELAND

SARAH DALY
B. 1888 WISCONSIN

JAMES CULLEN
B. 1812 COUNTY WEXFORD, IRELAND

CATHERINE CULLEN
B. 1853 WISCONSIN

BRIDGET FITZSIMMONS
B. 1825 IRELAND

FLANNERY FAMILY TREE

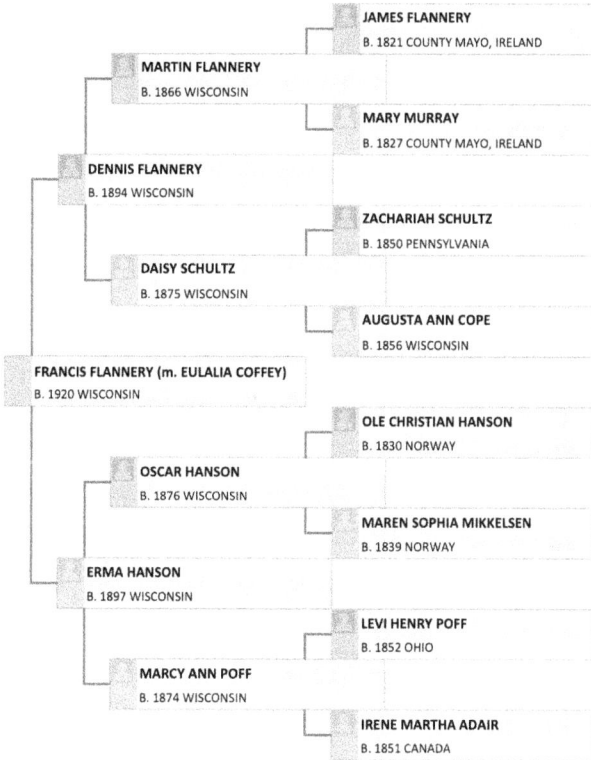

JAMES FLANNERY
B. 1821 COUNTY MAYO, IRELAND

MARTIN FLANNERY
B. 1866 WISCONSIN

MARY MURRAY
B. 1827 COUNTY MAYO, IRELAND

DENNIS FLANNERY
B. 1894 WISCONSIN

ZACHARIAH SCHULTZ
B. 1850 PENNSYLVANIA

DAISY SCHULTZ
B. 1875 WISCONSIN

AUGUSTA ANN COPE
B. 1856 WISCONSIN

FRANCIS FLANNERY (m. EULALIA COFFEY)
B. 1920 WISCONSIN

OLE CHRISTIAN HANSON
B. 1830 NORWAY

OSCAR HANSON
B. 1876 WISCONSIN

MAREN SOPHIA MIKKELSEN
B. 1839 NORWAY

ERMA HANSON
B. 1897 WISCONSIN

LEVI HENRY POFF
B. 1852 OHIO

MARCY ANN POFF
B. 1874 WISCONSIN

IRENE MARTHA ADAIR
B. 1851 CANADA

WATSON FAMILY TREE

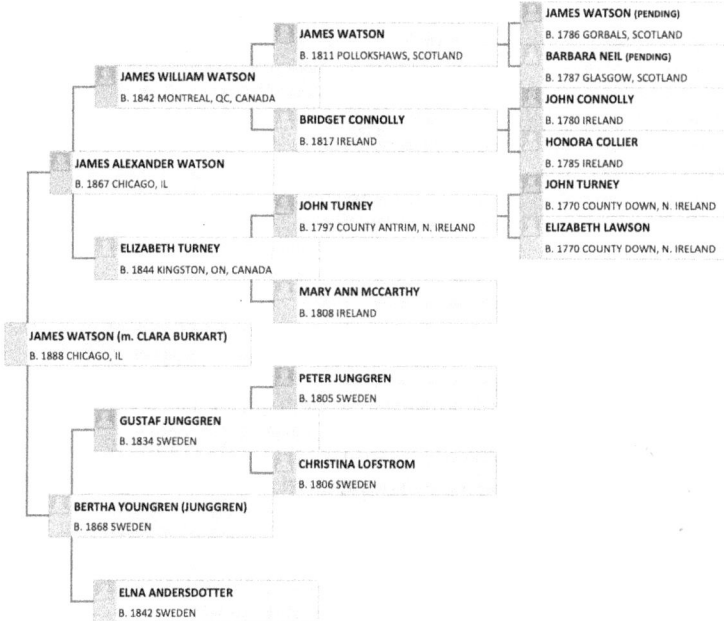

JAMES ALEXANDER WATSON
B. 1867 CHICAGO, IL

- **JAMES WILLIAM WATSON**
  B. 1842 MONTREAL, QC, CANADA
  - **JAMES WATSON**
    B. 1811 POLLOKSHAWS, SCOTLAND
    - **JAMES WATSON** (PENDING)
      B. 1786 GORBALS, SCOTLAND
    - **BARBARA NEIL** (PENDING)
      B. 1787 GLASGOW, SCOTLAND
  - **BRIDGET CONNOLLY**
    B. 1817 IRELAND
    - **JOHN CONNOLLY**
      B. 1780 IRELAND
    - **HONORA COLLIER**
      B. 1785 IRELAND
- **ELIZABETH TURNEY**
  B. 1844 KINGSTON, ON, CANADA
  - **JOHN TURNEY**
    B. 1797 COUNTY ANTRIM, N. IRELAND
    - **JOHN TURNEY**
      B. 1770 COUNTY DOWN, N. IRELAND
    - **ELIZABETH LAWSON**
      B. 1770 COUNTY DOWN, N. IRELAND
  - **MARY ANN MCCARTHY**
    B. 1808 IRELAND

JAMES WATSON (m. CLARA BURKART)
B. 1888 CHICAGO, IL

BERTHA YOUNGREN (JUNGGREN)
B. 1868 SWEDEN

- **GUSTAF JUNGGREN**
  B. 1834 SWEDEN
  - **PETER JUNGGREN**
    B. 1805 SWEDEN
  - **CHRISTINA LOFSTROM**
    B. 1806 SWEDEN
- **ELNA ANDERSDOTTER**
  B. 1842 SWEDEN

AUTHOR'S NOTE

Thank you so much for reading *Genealogy Tips & Quips*. If you enjoyed the book, I would greatly appreciate you taking the time to leave a review. Reviews encourage potential readers to give my stories a try, and I would love to hear your thoughts. My monthly newsletter features genealogy research advice, my latest news, and frequent giveaways! You can subscribe at www.elizawatson.com.

ABOUT ELIZA WATSON

Eliza Watson is a *USA Today* bestselling author and genealogist. Eliza's genealogy adventures have inspired two fiction series set in Ireland, Scotland, and England. She also writes a genealogy column for her monthly author newsletter and has written feature articles for genealogical societies. In 2013 she fulfilled her dream of owning a home in Ireland when she and her husband bought a renovated 1887 schoolhouse in her Coffey ancestors' townland. When Eliza isn't tracing her ancestry roots through Ireland or Scotland, she's at home working on her next novel, bouncing ideas off her husband, Mark, and her cats, Frankie and Sammy.

Connect with Eliza online:
www.elizawatson.com
www.facebook.com/ElizaWatsonAuthor
www.instagram.com/elizawatsonauthor

www.ingramcontent.com/pod-product-compliance
Lightning Source LLC
Chambersburg PA
CBHW060841280326
41934CB00007B/868